Reflec

A collection of short stories, observations,
memories and experiences as man & boy
in the 'wilds' of Sussex.

Mark Emery

This book is dedicated to my
parents Ray & Sandy Emery,
who taught me more than I ever knew,
also to my family, without whom,
I am nothing.

Contents

Contents

Acknowledgements

I would like to take this opportunity to thank a number of people for their help and support over the years, particularly the incredible support they have given me in the past few months, where I and our family have been through such a torrid time.

Firstly my family, my sister Carol, nephews Simon & Ollie, my niece Mel and my great niece Esme, my uncle Malcolm and cousin Gina in the USA and my cousin Margaret.

The following friends also need special mention and my eternal gratitude, for they have helped more than they could ever realise, Janet, Nicola, Nick, James, Derrick & Marlene, Oli & Row, Paul C, Barry G, Heather & Andy and last but not least Matthew, who in addition to his friendship, also provided me with some much needed and appreciated spiritual support and guidance.

I would also like to thank the nursing and support staff at both Worthing and Bognor Hospitals and the amazing staff from the Community Health Teams that have looked after me at home following my discharge from hospital.

At Worthing Hospital for looking after Mum in her final days and for me when I fell ill and spent so much time in their care, then at Bognor War Memorial Hospital where I was transferred from Worthing for rehabilitation and physiotherapy, you are amazing and I owe you all so much.

Foreword

Born to parents Ray & Sandy at the beginning of the 1970's, I spent the first four and half years of my life as an only child and being born to country folk, even at such a young age I spent a tremendous amount of time in the countryside.

Visits to family often involved a trek over the South Downs as my grandparents all lived in Steyning, so if we wanted to visit them, Mum & Dad had to cycle or walk over from Sompting, this involved either going up over the top of the hills via Steyning Bowl or along the old railway track that went from Shoreham to Steyning (now called the Downs Link) with me in a baby seat on the back of Dads bike.

A baby Sister arrived for me to torment in the mid 70's, in the main we got on fine as kids and still do to this day, do I still torment her?, you bet I do.

My Sister and I enjoyed a traditional country childhood, encouraged from an early age to go outside into the "wilds of Sussex" around Steyning & Sompting and to enjoy it, did it matter that we got filthy dirty covered in mud and crud?, not at all, all Mum used to say was *"we have a washing machine"*.

Most of our free time as kids was spent over the South Downs, building camps, lighting camp fires, hunting, walking and spending time on the farm with my grandfather and when we were not over the hills or in the woods, we could be found fishing on the beach at Shoreham or if Dad and I felt adventurous, we used to go to Dungeness in Kent, where he and I tried to catch a Cod or two (we never did get one) and Mum and my Sister spent time with relatives who lived on Romney Marsh.

We used to spend many weekends as a family in the woods at Steyning playing, climbing trees and using the Clematis vines as Tarzan Ropes (more on that later), all the time being subjected to the life that many kids envied, but unbeknown to us all this play was more than play, and it wasn't until much later in life that it dawned on me, that Mum & Dad were not only letting us play, but also taught us so much about life and the countryside and its wealth of resources that at the time we didn't take much notice of at all.

They also taught us just how cruel nature can be when it wants to be, but there are two sides to every coin and it did us no harm at all finding out about the sad things as well as the good things, it was all knowledge and unbeknownst to us there it was ingrained in our brains for future reference, all we had to do was unlock it.

When not out and about with Mum and Dad, I was often to be found over the Downs around home with my friends, still doing the same things like building camps, lighting fires, hunting etc. but without that adult supervision, we used to wander off for a day over the hills with a catapult made from a forked stick in our pocket, a Rambo Knife strapped to our belts, a box of matches, a packet of sausages and a cooking pot made from a baked bean tin with a bit of old wire coat hanger for a bail and nobody batted an eyelid, as long as we were back in time for dinner in the evening, we were fine and to be honest, all of our parents probably had a pretty good idea of where we were, oh how things have sadly changed for the worse,l where kids are often not allowed to go and explore on their own because of the idiots that are now prevalent in our society.

When I started secondary school, the country life went by the wayside for a few years as I discovered girls, well one one girl in particular, I also needed to work on my exams as I wanted to join the Royal Air Force, sadly despite staying on at school to get better grades for the trade I wanted to enter and leaving school with 18 exam passes at O Level, CSE & GCSE, I never did join the RAF, but instead went to work in the commercial aerospace industry, where I stayed for over 20 years.

It was during my time in the aerospace sector that I needed a release, so I went back to my roots and rediscovered all of the places I had been to when I was a kid, some of these places had remained relatively unchanged over the years, but other places had changed beyond recognition and it was during these visits to my old stomping grounds that I realised just exactly what Mum & Dad had been teaching us when we were kids, the places may have changed, I may have gotten a lot older, but the knowledge remained and of course, I had a whole new adventure to begin as I rediscovered the places, memories and adventures of my childhood.

As I write this im not only writing for prosperity, but also as a release, we lost Dad in November 2014 and in August 2022 we lost Mum to Cancer, three days after she passed away, I was admitted to hospital for just under seven weeks, unfortunately leaving all of the arrangements for Mum to my Sister and I am eternally grateful to her for doing what she did and continues to do for me to this day in day to day care whilst I wait to have bilateral knee replacement surgery, as im currently walking bone on bone in both knees which is as you can probably imagine, not that pleasant.

By writing these musings, I hope to find that all important mental release following a particularly hard episode in my life, that at the moment has no real end in sight.

It is through the following pages that I hope to be able to convey some of the stories and experiences of the countryside from my childhood and adult life, the stories are in no particular order and you will find yourself flitting from childhood to adulthood and back again.

I hope you enjoy reading them.

Dashers Seat

Sitting here on Dashers seat at the fishing ponds, I find myself surrounded by all manner of wildlife, a small vole occasionally darts across the path in front me on it's never ending search for food, where are those anglers and their supply of sweetcorn kernels when you need one?

The wild flowers are out in profusion and masses of Bumble and Honey Bees can be seen feeding on the Vetch & Trefoil that lines the paths around the area where I sit, there are butterflies everywhere, Marbled Whites, Meadow Browns, Speckled Woods, Comma, the occasional Holly Blue and the marvellous Red Admiral, all flitting away in the sunshine and settling often on the flowers to drink their nectar.

A movement out the corner of my eye reveals a Nuthatch searching the Oak in front of me, up and down the trunk it goes in its search for insects, a Carp jumping in the pond and landing with a splash soon frightens the bird off, although it doesn't phase the Moorhen and her chicks who just carry on as normal, the sky is alive with birds, a Buzzard circles overhead, lower down Swallows swoop and glide effortlessly over the surface of the pond getting a drink, before a flap of the wings sends them gracefully back up high, a profusion of small birds such as Blue & Great Tits, Dunnock, Starlings and Chaffinch busy themselves darting backwards and forwards over the ponds and through the trees, a Chiffchaf makes it's unique call in the near distance.

The pond is alive with Carp cruising around and shoals of small fish can be seen just sub surface, meanwhile thousands of fry erupt as a Crow flies overhead casting it's shadow on the water, over on the far bank a couple of anglers busy themselves in the glorious sunshine catching Roach, Rudd, Skimmers & Crucians and the odd Carp which gives one of them the run around for a few minutes.

It's not just about the angling, it's about being there and experiencing nature at it's finest that makes so many happy memories.

The Sit Tree

Everyone should have a Sit Tree, but what is a Sit Tree?

Simply put, its a place where you can go to be with your thoughts, to sit and reflect, think, watch nature, basically a retreat where you feel at ease and can relax and let the pressures of modern life melt away for a few hours.

The calming effects of trees and woodland on the human soul has been well documented and there is a wealth of information on the subject out there, both on the internet and in those old fashioned places called *"Libraries"*, so I will not go into that here, but leave it up to you, the reader, to research for yourself.

A Sit Tree can be any tree of your choice, large or small, perhaps a majestic Oak or Beech in a park or woodland close to home or as mine is, a solitary knarly old Ash on the side of hill about a mile or so from my home.

My tree is on the west facing slope of the hill behind the house and it stands guard over the valley below, with the Iron Age Hill Fort of Cissbury Ring perching on top of the hill a few short miles away forming the valley wall on the far side of this wide expanse of Sussex countryside.

Having explained what a Sit Tree is and its purpose, I thinks its time we paid a short visit to my tree.

With a shoulder bag packed with a few essential items such as tea, sandwiches and a pair of binoculars, I start my journey to the tree along a winding lane that has seen the feet of man and beast for centuries, but more of that in another Chapter.

Once at the tree I sit beneath it, enjoying the dappled shade of the canopy and using its trunk as a convenient back rest.

Unpacking my bag I pour myself a well earned and much needed cup of tea and devour a cheese and tomato sandwich, well I do need to replace the energy I used getting here.

I do wonder why though, that any sandwich with tomato in it always tastes so much better out of doors, perhaps that's something I can ponder this afternoon as sit here.

Having refreshed myself and gotten myself comfortable, I lean further back against the tree and let my mind wander whilst the magnificence of the landscape washes over me and takes my worries and woes with it like a leaf tumbling on the surface of a fast flowing stream.

Its not long before I start to feel part of the landscape and following the disturbance of my arrival, nature itself is starting to settle down and return to some sort of normality, with birds, animals and insects all starting to accept me and return to the vicinity.

The first to arrive are the insects, butterflies, bees, beetles and a solitary Dragon Fly buzz around me as if they are investigating this recent addition to their environment, on the ground around me all manner of beetles, spiders and other equally as interesting and beautiful bugs and beasties carry on their daily struggle for survival, with some taking advantage of the crumbs from my sandwich and the dregs from my tea as a gift from heaven in the daily search for food and water, only for some of them following a free feed, to be consumed themselves by the miniature predators in their equally as hard daily struggle for survival.

I digress slightly, but I have always found it moderately amusing when people say there is nothing happening and the countryside is a barren wilderness, there is always something happening, you just have to take the time to slow down and become aware of your surroundings to see the big wide world that's literally right under your feet.

Back to the tree, now feeling totally relaxed under the tree and despite the war that rages around me, I take some deep breaths of the fresh, enriching country air, close my eyes and let my senses absorb nature as she lets me into her realm.

Almost immediately I hear the song of a Dunnock in the branches above me, the cooing of the Wood Pigeon and down in the valley below the familiar clack, clack of the Cock Pheasant reverberating over the fields.

I can hear the sheep and cattle on the farm in the distance, these sounds being interrupted by the noise of the farmer on his huge blue tractor as he draws a rattling harrow over the land.

I'm at peace with myself and my surroundings, but not for long, as the peace is shattered by the alarm calls of the small birds, I open my eyes and have to wait a few seconds for them to adjust to the light, before a swift movement to my right betrays what caused the serenity to be shattered.

A male Sparrowhawk is on the prowl, with it's distinctive flap, flap, glide flight, but he is not having it all his own way today, his presence has alerted the local Crows, who now mock him on the wing with a constant barrage of dives and attacks, eventually the Sparrowhawk decides enough is enough, no food here today and he flies off to what he hopes will be a quieter and perhaps more productive area.

With the area settling down again after the hubbub of a few moments ago, its time for another cuppa, but before I can even pour myself a drink, an absolutely beautiful Peacock butterfly alights on my leg and sits there with wings outstretched showing off the dazzling colours and patterns on its wings, the tea can wait as I sit there mesmerised by the butterflies beauty.

Its not long before it decides my leg is not as comfortable a roost as it first thought and it rises and flutters off on the gentle breeze to join its friends on the Hemp Agrimony a few short paces away.

With the butterfly gone I can now sup on my tea which hits the spot a treat, just as im finishing my tea I notice a movement in the field below me, I carefully raise my binoculars and focus on the area.

To my amazement, there, right in front of me is a Roe Deer Doe, now I feel part of the landscape, if she had any inkling I was there, if she had seen me move or scented me on the breeze, she would never have been so bold as to venture out into the open and away from the security of the brush and undergrowth from which she undoubtedly appeared.

I've seen hundreds if not thousands of Deer in the wild in my years travelling and exploring the South Downs, but its always a treat to see another, then suddenly she raises her head and as quickly as she arrived, she flees at top speed, only stopping to look back when she felt safe from whatever it was that spooked her, the answer to that question is soon answered as the farmer speeds over the fields on his quad bike doing his rounds.

Time is getting on now and its about time I thought about heading back home, perhaps just one more cup of tea before I do.

Refreshed once again, I pack away my belongings and make sure the only things I have left behind are footprints and a few crumbs from my sandwich, both of which will be erased by mother nature by morning, leaving little or no trace that I was ever here.

There may be no trace of me, but the lasting effects of a short visit to my tree will be with me forever, the Peacock butterfly on my leg, the Sparrowhawk being heckled, The Roe Deer plus all the other wonders of the natural world have cleared my mind, my soul feels cleansed and I have a feeling of tranquillity, that for me, I can only achieve in nature, preparing me to face the hustle and bustle of the modern world once again.

So, all I can say is this, go and find yourself a Sit Tree, sit calm and peaceful and let yourself connect with nature, you'll be glad you did.

Surprise

One of the biggest problems that kids face these days is confrontation from adults whenever they are out and about, be this down town or out in the countryside, sure they know they are up to no good, heck we did things as kids when our parents were not around that we knew could get us in trouble if we got caught, but so have all kids for millennia, its nothing new, but it is amazing how their attitude changes when you converse with them rather than having a go, and after all, I would be a hypocrite for having a go at kids for doing something that I did myself when I was their age.

I work in the woods as part of my living and on one occasion I had a couple of colleagues with me, after a days work under the leafy canopy, we were walking out of the work area and slowly making our way home.

On our journey out of the woodland we could smell the characteristic odour of a wood fire, so we went to investigate, as to our knowledge we were the only people in this area on this day.

We followed our noses and happened across a group of lads having a few beers, sitting around a roaring fire, a few things sprang to mind straight away, firstly, they were under age drinking, secondly, the woods are private and they should not have been there and thirdly, fires are out of the question there, as it's part of a SSSI.

These kids must have pooped themselves when out of the blue three big burly blokes dressed in green, with rucksacks and axes appeared out of nowhere, we made a bit of noise on our way towards them to let them know we were around, but even so, they looked a bit shocked and you could tell by their faces they were expecting to get shouted at, they were stoked up and ready to retaliate in kind, but instead of having a go and creating an unnecessary and potentially dangerous situation, bearing in mind we had a number of sharp cutting tools with us, we just asked if we could we use their fire to put our kettle on, as we fancied a cup of tea.

This immediately diffused any situation as it was totally opposite to what they were expecting, in the end we sat there for about an hour or so and had a really nice chat with them, we explained what we did and the work we were doing in the woods, showed them a few easy countryside skills and just told them that they shouldn't really be there, let alone be having a fire, no animosity was received or given, after a while we packed up our stuff and bid them farewell.

We went back the next day expecting to find an awful mess, but to these lads credit, the fire pit had been cleared away as best they could, there was no rubbish anywhere and we never saw them in these woods again.

Now whether it was the shock of three blokes appearing out of nowhere or because we sat down and actually spoke to them rather than got all uppity and shouting at them we will never know, but I bet if we had had a go at them, the place would have been left in a right state just to spite us.

Just goes to show that if you treat people, of all ages, with the decency and respect you would expect to receive, rather than getting your undies in an almighty twist, then many problems simply do not happen.

I would like to think that those lads learnt an important lesson that day, and you never know one day, I might be in the woods and they come over and ask to share my camp fire for a brew.

The Copse

At the end of the road and over the turnip field lies The Copse, the place of many an adventure as a boy.

Some of my earliest memories of this small woodland go back to when I was a mere nipper and when we were just allowed to go out and play, explore and have fun on our own without the worries of a modern day society weighing heavily on our parents minds, they of course knew exactly where we were and we were never too far from home if help was needed, but just far enough away to be in our own world of wonder and discovery.

The Copse, although not a proper copse, is a small naturally seeded woodland that grows on the site of an old quarry, this small woodland has Wych Elm, Horse Chestnut, Sycamore, Hazel & Elder growing in it and as I remember it, the ground surface was covered in lush green grass.

To small boys, who at the time were unaware of the species of trees and basically didn't really care about such things, the trees provided us with all manner of fallen branches with which we would build dens and camps, we never cut greenwood, as none of us had ever heard of the small folding saws that are so freely available these days, nor did any of us think to take a bow saw with us, we had our pocket knives and a few of us had our "Rambo" style knives, all of which were as blunt as a butter knife, but we knew no better and were happy, so it didn't matter.

Of course some days fate intervened and one particular visit saw us "discover" a huge pile of wooden fence posts and rails, well to a group of country boys this was a pennies from heaven moment and the pile of fencing materials were just perfect for making a tree house.

So we ran back home and raided my friends dads workshop for six inch nails, hammers and anything else we thought would come in useful for our construction project, quite what his dad thought when he came home from work and went to his workshop to see his tools and equipment missing, well I guess only my friend can answer that.

Laden down with tools and equipment we went back to the woods and set to making the best tree house we had ever seen, the noise of hammering and excited voices must have carried over the fields, but nobody came to see what we were up to, after a few hours our master piece was complete, a triangular platform made from the sturdy fence posts had been erected between three trunks of the tree we had selected, the floor being made from half round posts and rails and it was easily big enough for a couple of us to sit on.

The tree house lasted a few weeks until one eventful day we went back to the woods only to find our masterpiece of modern design had gone, nothing was left.

Undoubtedly the farmer had come down to the copse to do a days fencing around the adjacent fields, only to find all of his materials had gone, it probably didn't take him long to figure out where it was, he had disassembled our tree house as carefully as we had built it and removed all of the timber so it could be used for its proper task.

Only now years later, can I imagine the air turning blue as he found his materials missing and the additional work we had created for him to take the tree house apart, prising nails with a crowbar and muttering *"bloody kids"* under his breath.

Our tree house was gone, but there was a nice new fence around the field.

On another trip to our wood, we found a dead rabbit laying on the side path that led to the copse, knowing no better we picked it up and discovering that it smelt fine, we thought we would have a bit of a cook up.

We gathered armfuls of dead nettle stems, small dead twigs and a few larger pieces of wood and lit a small fire at the base of one of the big trees, it was always very exciting to have a fire, especially as we knew we shouldn't really be doing it, so with fire lit and it burning well, we put our bunny on the fire, of course none of us had thought to skin and gut it first.

Being fairly excitable small boys, we were soon distracted by something else and seeing that the fire had died down, we just threw a load of dry stuff on the top and went off to do something else.

A short(ish) while later we returned to our bunny barbecue, only to find the rabbit was gone, in our haste to go and play elsewhere we had put far too much fuel on the fire and not only cooked the bunny, but had cremated it, nothing was left, as far as I can remember we didn't even find a bone, not that we really looked too hard in the smouldering ashes.

We never did get our bunny dinner, which was probably just as well as heaven only knows what diseases would have been waiting for us, so in good old country boy fashion, we put the fire out in the only way small boys do, kicked a load of dirt over the top and went home for a proper dinner.

The copse continued to be our playground, school room and bolt hole for many years, until exams and girls took precedence and not necessarily in that order.

The copse unfortunately was devastated during the great storm of 1987, all bar half a dozen or so of the large trees were felled by the wind, after the storm I went back up there to view the destruction and could not believe what I was seeing, a complete jumble of uprooted trees and smashed branches.

The farm did go up and clean it all up and I can remember speaking to the farmer and him telling me about the carnage around the farm, the storm didn't spare anything, lovely old, majestic tress gone in a heartbeat, some having taken hundreds of years to grow and now reduced to splintered fire wood, it was tragic.

The scar of the storm can still be seen in the copse today, gone are the remains of the big trees, the holes left by their root plates are still visible, but the grassy ground of my youth has gone and its now just a bare, flint and chalk surface, very little ground cover now grows apart from Ground Ivy, Nettles, Cleavers and Lords & Ladies, although the woodland edge is full of all manner of wild edible plants to those who know what they are looking at, not that I forage these as there are far too many dogs around.

The trees are slowly making a come back and the farm has in recent years, mainly due to being under new management, begun to replant the copse with new trees, but as is always the case when planting trees, you are not planting them for yourself, but for the next generation, so I hope that in fifty to sixty years from now when im pushing up the daisies, that a group of small boys discover the copse and find the adventure we found there when we were their age

NB: I refer to the word 'copse' as this is how it is pronounced by us old yokels, according to the legendary countryman Jack Hargreaves, the older ordnance maps show it as being spelt as both copse and coppice with coppice being shown on the oldest maps, so that's probably the correct historical spelling, but its still pronounced as copse regardless of how its spelt, copse is the area, coppicing is what you do.

Secret Camp

About half a mile from home, which was about as far as we would wander at the time, there was and still is to this day, a small overgrown area adjacent to where two footpaths join.

This place was totally unexplored and a complete jumble of Bramble, Dog Rose, Stinging Nettles and other nasties, i.e. just the right place to build a secret camp.

In we went, full of thorns and stung to bits we broke through into a clearing, this place was perfect, it had a boundary that no sane person would try and break through, a nice grassy clearing in the middle and a few small trees and shrubs that we could shelter under if it rained – paradise found.

One afternoon on the way home from school we nipped into the grocery shop and bought a packet of sausages and a few cans of Barbican (alcohol free lager), these were stashed in our school bags and we quickly made our way home, got changed, grabbed our *"Survival Kits"* and headed out into the wilds of the Sussex countryside to our new camp.

Once there we quickly set to getting a fire going so we could cook our sausages, our cans of Barbican were cracked open and we sat there around the fire drinking alcohol free lager and waiting for the bangers to cook, ahh we knew how to live.

With sausages cooked and consumed, Barbican downed it was time to go home for dinner, so we extinguished the fire using the by product of too much alcohol free lager, pushed our way out of our secret camp and wandered back home.

After dinner we all met up again and decided to go back to the secret camp, only to find the fire had not been put out quite as well as we had thought, some of the larger pieces of wood were now only smouldering dogs, the dead grass around the fire pit had caught too and what was a small fire area before, was now a good four to five foot in diameter.

In the distance we could hear the familiar Nee Nah of an emergency service siren, from our vantage point we could see the hill road and saw a Fire Engine with lights flashing and siren going turn off the road and onto the farm track that led directly towards us, we didn't need prompting and legged it.

We went back a few days later and could see the Fire Brigade has properly extinguished our fire pit, the ground had been raked over, the log dogs and fire wood was all spread out and soaking wet and our secret camp was no longer a secret.

That was the closest I had ever been to setting the South Downs on fire and we never did go back to that camp during childhood, I did try to get in there many years later, but its now so overgrown that its absolutely impossible to get into.

The Angler

I've fished for as long as I can remember, starting off sea fishing from the beach at Shoreham, then for the last 30 years or so being a freshwater angler.

Now there is a difference between a fisherman and an angler, and I consider myself to be the latter, as one of my friends once said *"a fisherman catches fish, but an angler not only catches fish, but also takes in and appreciates the wider environment around them"*, and like in the previous chapter where my best days shooting didn't involve taking a single shot, the best days fishing can be a day when you catch very little, but the events of the day make it special, be that seeing a rare bird or animal, to having and enjoying really good company.

I have many experiences in my angling career, far too many to convey in this tome as they would fill an entire volume on their own, perhaps that will be my next set of scribblings, so

I will limit it here to a few stand out moments from my early days as an angler.

One of my earliest memories of going fishing is when I was probably no more than six or seven years old, Dad and I were on the beach at Shoreham fishing for anything that we could get.

Dad would cast out for as despite me being very enthusiastic, I was just not big enough to to cast a 12ft beachcaster and four ounce lead out far enough, but I was able to bring the tackle back in when I could, back then we used Dad's fibreglass rods which were seriously heavy compared to the carbon rods we later used and his Intrepid Sea Streak multiplier reels, which I still have, there was no such thing as a level wind back then, so I was always instructed on how to retrieve the tackle and lay the line level on the spool, im sure I cocked it up more than once, but unless it was a right mess, Dad didn't normally say anything.

As we sat there on the shingle, the rod tip rattled, Dad was up like a shot, he wound down to the fish and struck into it, then he passed the rod to me and I started winding in, the line felt heavy, so we knew it was something a bit better than the usual Flounder or Plaice we normally caught, into the light surf the fish came, then as the waves receded, there on the beach was what I called a Skate, in retrospect it was probably a small Thornback or Undulate Ray, but to me it was a huge Skate and that was the first fish I can ever remember catching and what a way to open my account, even all these years later I can still see that fish on the beach and remember the excitement of catching it, after that I was quite literally – hooked!

We used to fish on a regular basis, both as a family and just Dad and myself, summer, winter, day and night we always gave it go, we used to make the occasional trip to Dungeness in the winter time trying for a Cod or two, we never did get one, just Pouting, Whiting and Weavers. The trip east was always a family affair as we used to combine it with a trip to see Aunt Mary, then after a cuppa Dad and I would disappear to Dungeness for a few hours fishing behind the power station, while Mum and my Sister stayed at Mary's, then when Dad and I returned back empty handed, we would pack the car up and travel back home, exhausted, but happy.

Of course to go fishing you need bait and that was always a fun thing for Dad and I to do, he would show me the correct way to dig Lugworm and Red Rag, always being careful to backfill the hole as we went and me being told on repeated occasions, until it finally sank in, not to pull the worms out but break the sand or mud away from them so you don't pull the worms in half.

If we wanted soft or peeler crab we didn't bother rock pooling like many did, we were up the river where we would raid the burrows made by the crabs in the side of the bank, well I say "we", I mean "Dad", he used to just shove his hands into these deep, foreboding holes in the bank and come out with a crab in his hand, im sure he got nipped quite often as he rummaged around in these holes, but if he did he never said or showed that he had.

I now know from experience that it really hurts when a crab nipped you, but back then I never quite had the courage to put my hands blindly into those holes knowing what lay at the other end, so that was always Dad's job.

One bait digging trip saw us all venture a fair way upstream on the river to a spot where at low tide a sand (mud) bank appeared, the area was not a nice sand, more of a stinking black, oozing mud, but it was one of the best spots we knew for some seriously big Red Rag and in quantity.

Due to the nature of the bank, we had it instilled in us that we never dug close to the sides of the river so as to not undermine them, so we always dug a little way out and towards the waters edge.

On this particular trip we were accompanied by Mum & Sister, now this area we were at for the bait although being a good bait digging spot, was also a bit dangerous as it is pock marked with areas of very, very soft mud that would trap the unwary, quickly and easily, so we were all told not to venture off in case we went straight into one of these areas of stinking sinking mud.

So my Sister being my Sister, wanders off over the foreshore in her little red wellies, it wasn't long before she was stuck in the soft mud and was sinking, not happy with just being stood in this stinking black goo, she then decided to sit down in it for good measure.

Mum & Dad were not happy and rushed over to get her out of the predicament she found herself in, if I remember correctly when we went home she was taken out of her mucky clothes and was sat on an old sack in the back of the car so she didn't transfer the black goo to the car seats. We laugh at it now, but the repercussions of that day could have been disastrous.

Other bait digging excursions were not quite so eventful, there was the time Dad and I were digging Rag at the Toll Bridge which started off as just a normal trip to dig bait, that was until Dad saw a shoal of large Grey Mullet grazing the sea weed on the bridge stanchions, bait digging was temporarily suspended whilst Dad crept up the fish with the bait fork in his hand like and Aboriginal with his fishing spear, closer and closer Dad got until he was within striking distance, a fish appeared by the bridge, Dad was poised to strike!

Then an explosion of fins and steel as Dad launched the fork into the water towards the Mullet, the fork entered the water, missed the fish and embedded itself squarely in the bottom of the river, the fish were gone, the fork was retrieved and as our heart rates calmed down from the thrill of the hunt, we gathered ourselves together and went back to the Rag beds.

The fish had been well and truly spooked and didn't return all the time we were there, still, if you never try these things, you will never know.

I think it was on this trip or one shortly after that Dad told me about the times he used to go spear fishing in the muddy channels that lined the lower reaches of the river.

He used to walk the channels just before low tide with his fish spear, that had started life as a javelin used in field athletics, I can remember him saying that you travelled slowly and with purpose, trying not to stir the bottom up too much so you could see the fish on the mud and that when you aimed at the fish you never took aim directly at it, but went just in front of it and that is when I learnt all about refraction and a it was a far better lesson on the subject than I ever received in Physics class at school.

Our fishing wasn't limited to rod and line though, on a family summer holiday we had taken in Wales, we found ourselves walking along the banks of a very scenic Welsh river, when Mum & Dad saw the familiar shapes of Trout out in the water, we all carefully sat down a short distance back from the river whilst Dad crawled like a Commando towards the rivers edge, Dad was going Trout Tickling.

We sat there motionless as Dad did his thing and watched in amazement as he placed his hand and forearm into the cool waters of the river and waited with his hand outstretched.

It wasn't long before the familiar shape of a fish appeared and after a wait that seemed like ages slowly glided over Dads hand and then just sat there as Dads fingers gently caressed the belly of the fish, he didn't attempt to catch it mind, he just showed us how it was done, now it all sounds very simple and easy to do, until you try it.

I moved slowly and deliberately towards Dad at the waters edge, I lay down and put my small quivering hand into the water where thankfully there was a convenient rock for me to rest it upon. I don't know how long I was there waiting but eventually a Trout appeared and with my heart thumping, I waited and waited for the fish to move closer towards me, eventually it lost its wariness and cautiously nestled over my hand, I was now a Trout Tickler too.

For a small boy and indeed as an adult years later, its a magical feeling using nothing but your hands and your guile, plus a bucket full of patience as a wild creature approaches and rests on your hand, knowing that the slightest wrong movement and it would gone for good

Enough of holidays and learning how to go poaching, it's back to the beach and one of our regular trips out to Shoreham for a bit of night fishing, I really enjoyed the night trips with Dad, not just for the fishing, but because it always meant a late night.

Armed with peeler and soft crab, plus a bucketful of worms, we were armed and primed to catch some Bass. Mum & Dad used to tell me of the times they used to go Bass fishing at Pagham Harbour where anything they caught that was under six or seven pounds they would put back as it was too small, the ones they kept would get put into Nan's sink when they got home and there the fish lay waiting to greet Nan first thing in the morning with their big glassy eyes .

We went back to Pagham many years after Mum & Dad had last fished it to see if we could get to the spot they used to fish, unfortunately for us that area was now part of a nature reserve and fishing was no longer allowed – a great shame.

Back to Shoreham, Dad and I had both tackled and baited up and cast our rigs out, a short time later my rod tip rattled like something possessed, I struck into the bite and felt the fish on the other end, it was nothing big, just a small school Bass, far too small to keep so back it went with the instruction to tell its bigger brothers to come and play. Not long after Dad had a very soft bite on his worm rig, he struck and his rod arched over, just a dead weight, no fight at all.

When he bought the tackle up the beach all we could see in the dim light of the hurricane lamp was a mass of seaweed, Dad cleared the weed away to reveal to what I openly exclaimed to be an old sock, because that's exactly what it looked like, an old, rotten, misshapen, woollen sock, then it moved and Dad picked up what was and still is the biggest Sole I've ever seen, it was huge – some sock.

Dad and I had many night trips, summer and winter, the summer trips going for Bass which we caught plenty of, but never anything really big as Mum and Dad had done in the past, the winter trips were for Codling, which we never did catch as the stocks had been decimated by commercial boats, thankfully these days the Cod stocks have recovered and Codling are quite often caught off the beach again.

One overriding memory of winter nights on the beach, was it being so cold that your breath froze on your eyebrows making us look like polar explorers.

On the opposite side of the coin were lazy summer afternoons as a family on the beach, one trip that still stands out is from a time that saw Mum in hospital recovering from an operation, so Dad took my Sister and I fishing for a couple of hours before we went to the hospital to see Mum.

We went to what we called the long beach, as it was only a short trip we had the minimum of tackle with us, but in the end we called this already short trip even shorter, as we were catching so many Mullet that we got bored, yup, one of those red letter days that every angler wants and looks forward to, but when it happened, we packed up and went early, anglers can be a strange breed.

Easter Monday

Every Easter Monday Dad and I used to walk from home in Sompting to my grandparents house and my Dads childhood home in Steyning.

To get there we followed an ancient track way that lays at the end of the road we live in, the track, as its commonly known these days can be traced backed hundreds, if not thousands of years and I often wonder how many feet have traversed its stony surface over the millennia and how the landscape, environment and ecology has changed over the centuries.

Our journey always started with packing up Dads old blue canvas rucksack with essential supplies, flask of tea, tomato sandwiches, jackets and probably whatever items I felt were essential to me, that I probably never even looked at once we were under way.

The track runs north to south and at the time these journeys were undertaken it intersected a monoculture landscape of wheat, in fact every field you could see on this farm was wheat, it wasn't until we got a few miles further up the track and on top of the Downs that the crops changed, there were still seas of wheat, but on the neighbouring farms you could see large expanses of lush green grass with flocks of sheep interspersed around them, just occasionally you would see the odd herd of beef cattle, but it was mainly wheat and sheep.

Starting our journey on top of the small rise that leads to the track from home under sunny Spring skies, we look down a long winding path that for a youngster seems to be never ending as it winds its way into the near distance, the reality is our objective is but a few short miles away, but when you have little legs, it felt like a marathon.

Walking down the path there are lots of things in the hedgerow that Dad took great pride in me telling about, the Rose Hips that he used to collect when he was a child himself during the war and how they used to make a syrup from them as that was their only source of vitamin c, as oranges were simply not available, a few steps further down and he shows me the bramble bushes alluding to their bountiful blackberry harvest later in the year.

Off to the side is a Sycamore tree and I root around in the leaf litter underneath trying to find some Sycamore seeds that I can throw up in the air and watch as they float down like miniature helicopters, but they are all gone, the field mice and birds have had the lot over winter.

We carry on down the track, past the old flint barn, which is sadly no longer there, then past the water works, before heading up the slight rise in the path as we head northwards, before too long we are at the junction in the track where another path joins from the east, we have not walked more than half a mile, but its time for a short rest on the old rotting log and strangely enough right next to the area where just a few short years in the future I nearly set fire to the South Downs.

We carry on northwards, the Elm hedge to our west slowly peters out and we are left looking over the wheat fields towards Sompting Woods clinging onto the side of the hill on the opposite side of the valley, those woods were a place that we never did go to much when we were kids, they always seemed a bit spooky and there was the very high risk of getting caught in there by the landowner.

We carry on walking and chatting about things like lads and dads do, Dad still pointing out different things like wild flowers, perhaps a bunny or two on the edge of the field ahead and the wild birds, although like the number you see on the same walk today, back then if you saw a Buzzard it was a sight to behold, these days through conservation measures they are so common, that you rarely look up that often when you hear one, a positive change to the countryside for once.

Its not long before we go over a slight rise that bends to the right and to one of my favourite stops on these walks with Dad, a small exposed chalk face on the side of the hill means I can go fossil hunting, all I ever found were small bits of shell, but to think im the first person to ever see these shells, not to mention they are millions of years old, they always did and still do fascinate me, Dad like every time we have stopped here before has to drag me away as I could explore the chalk for hours, but if we don't move we wont get to Steyning on time.

Just up the path we walk past what is now my sit tree and now face our first big decision as the path comes to a T junction, do we go left to Cissbury Ring & Chanctonbury, otherwise known as the long route or do we go right and the short route via Steyning bowl, decisions, decisions.

This time we take the long route, no wonder Dad was keen to get me away from fossil hunting.

Turning left we continue our journey along the track , we go down the hill and past the spot in the bottom of this very small valley that always, no matter what the weather, seems to be wet, climbing up the slope on the other side we soon come to the road between Steyning and Sompting and carefully cross to the other side.

We are now on a path that's a lot less trodden, the grass is longer on each side of the path and Dad says if we are lucky we might see an Adder or Grass Snake, I cant remember if we ever did, but the excitement of possibility was always there, a few hundred yards further down the track we come to what to young boy can only be described as a cliff face, the steepness of this one part of the track seemed immense and far too dangerous to go down, even to this day when I take this walk, this part of the track is still incredibly steep and great care is taken going down it, still id rather go down it, than climb up it.

Down we go, Dad telling me to be careful as the last thing we want are grazed knees or twisted ankles, we get to the bottom, turn and look up at this slope, did we really just come down that, we are brave soldiers today.

We walk ever westward towards the dominating figure in the landscape that is Cissbury Ring Iron Age Hill Fort and Neolithic Flint Mines, we don't have time to go and explore it today unfortunately, although we are not exactly rushing either, as we head towards the Fort we see the remains of an ancient Dew Pond, which thankfully after years and years of neglect has been fully restored in recent years by Sompting Estate, it's now an oasis in the landscape for birds and animals, although at the time of this particular journey it wasn't even a muddy hole.

Dad and I are now at the foot of Cissbury Ring where we take a short break by the old barn before heading off toward our next objective of Chanctonbury Ring which we can see in the distance, itself an Iron Age Hill Fort, but also surrounded by prehistoric monuments such as Bronze age Cross Dykes and remains of burial barrows right up to the relatively modern Roman remains in the middle of the ring.

As we head towards Chanctonbury we can hear a thunderous rumble to our left, Dad knows exactly what it is but doesn't say, im left wondering until in the distance I see a couple of race horses from Josh Giffords stables thundering down the gallops towards us just the other side of the fence line, two magnificent beasts, rippling with muscle and sinew go racing past with their jockeys seeming to be holding on for dear life, I watch in total amazement as they race past and disappear into the distance.

The excitement over, Dad and I continue on our way along the flinty path towards dear old Chanctonbury, Dad all the time pointing out things along the way, not just stuff close by, but also way off in the distance, from our vantage point on top of the Downs we can see Brighton and the Seven Sisters in the east, to Bognor and the masts at Goodwood to the west, the magnificence of Cissbury Ring lays to our south and Chanctonbury is ever closer to the north.

As we near Chanctonbury we decide not to go to the actual Ring today, but instead start to descend through the trees on the north slope of the hill, today we act sensible and take the footpath to the bottom of the hill, normally we would go straight down through the woodland on our backsides, sliding down the steep slope and trying to navigate away from the trees so we don't crash, but time is getting on and we still have a little way to go, so the safer option it is, again as we walk down through the trees Dad is constantly pointing things out, plants, trees, wildlife, a broken birds egg lays on the ground in front of me and he asks if I know what bird it came from, I have little or no idea and don't even hazard a guess.

He tells me to look up, I do this and above me in the branches is the unmistakeable haphazard nest of a Wood Pigeon, therefore its stands to reason that the egg in front of me is a Pigeon egg, Dad says im right and he seems pleased that his teachings are at long last sinking in.

We continue down the path, looking and learning all the time, then we get to the swinging ropes, now anyone who has been to Chanctonbury will know the swinging ropes, we are not going any further until I've had some fun on the ropes, so we stop and we both play on the ropes for a while, it comes as a welcome rest stop before the final push into Steyning and Nan's house.

After a while we decide its time to move on, so we continue on the last leg of our journey, we turn right towards Steyning, go through the farmyard of Chanctonbury Farm and follow the path along the bottom of the hill, we see Wiston House to our left, a huge country pile and where my Nan worked in the 1930's, Dad tells me about the times he went there when he was a child and the magnificence of the Minstrels Gallery in the house.

We walk along the field edge as Wiston House grows smaller behind us and are heading towards Round Robin and the stream, soon we are walking down Mouse Lane and im enjoying splashing in and kicking up the water that bubbles up through the road from the natural springs that only ever dry up in the hot weather of summer.

We are now in Steyning, one final stop before we reach our destination and that's by The Star pub, not for a drink, but to look in the stream that runs alongside to see if there are any Trout to be seen, none today unfortunately.

Ten minutes later we are at Nan's where we meet up with Mum & my Sister who have driven over from home to collect the intrepid explorers, Dad is met with a nice fresh cup of tea, I've got a glass of squash and a big slice of Nan's home made cake, filled with home made jam, made from fruits harvested from the garden.

Not long after we are on our way home, im absolutely shattered, my legs and feet hurt, but my head is spinning with details of everything I've seen and experienced today, im going to sleep well tonight, what shall I dream of, fossil hunting, race horses, swinging ropes or the next adventure that Dad and I go on?

The Horseshoe

The Horseshoe is a heavily wooded hillside on the outskirts of Steyning, locals will know both the upper and lower horseshoe, these being the paths that run around the top of the hill and the bottom of the hill respectively.

We used to spend loads of time here when we were growing up, as did Mum and Dad in their childhoods, although back then the hillside was fairly open grassland that was interspersed with with Hazel coppice and large Beech trees and not the woodland of today where the hillside is covered in Ash and Sycamore with an understorey of Hazel, Elder and the occasional Field Maple, there are still a few big Beech trees here and they have stood guard for hundreds of years and certainly they have looked over previous generations of our family as they played and worked here in years gone by.

Dad used to convey the times he and his friends used to come up to the horseshoe and play, cook twisters over a small fire, go birds nesting for the eggs (illegal now), and the time one of his friends had an egg in his mouth so he could carry it down safely after having just liberated it from the Rooks nest high in the tree, but unfortunately missed his footing on the way down and crushed the raw egg between his jaws as he slipped, not that Dad would have laughed (much) at his friends predicament or Dad being sent up with a sack by Grandad to the area that was wooded to collect leaf mould for the garden, even now there is no better mulch or fertiliser for the garden, if you can get permission to take it, after all, by taking it, you are removing habitat from the woods, but things were very much different back then and nobody batted an eyelid and the science of ecology had not even been born, but the country folk, understood how things worked, even if they didn't have a label for it.

As a family we used to go to the Horseshoe at least a couple of weekends each month, we used to park the car up by the chalk pit and then walk down from there to the Horseshoe through the remains of the old quarry.

To get to the upper path you basically just turned left, but we didn't often go up there, as the walk up was exhausting to say the least and there really were not too many places up there where we could go and play, whereas the lower path was much more fun, even getting there was fun as once through the old quarry workings we stood on the top of a slope that was covered in long grass and this was just perfect for grass sledging.

Now what is grass sledging?, well simply put its sledging on grass without snow, no sledge though, our steeds for this little adventure were old fertiliser sacks that we had got from Grandad at the farm, these conveniently packed down fairly small and were of course light to carry, so they could be packed away in a bag nicely when not in use, of course they could also be used later to carry back leaf mould for the garden.

Standing at the top of the slope, we would place the sacks down on the ground, sit on them, then with a gentle shove from Mum or Dad we would thunder down the grassy slope like greased lighting, picking up speed all the time and with absolutely no control, the sacks had a mind of their own each little bump meant a change in direction and with no runners, these things were were free to rotate, so quite often we would end up going down the hill sideways or even backwards.

Now stopping was the fun part, at the bottom of the slope was a Blackthorn & Hawthorn hedge, we had no brakes and were going at some considerable speed, the only way to stop in time before you hit this line of hurt was to literally roll over onto the grass, of course momentum meant you didn't necessarily stop with much dignity, usually you carried on for a few yards or so in a blur of arms and legs as you tumbled those last few yards towards the hedge, nine times out of ten we stopped before the hedge, but sometimes it hurt.

Picking ourselves up off the floor, covered in grass, mud and whatever else we had rolled through, we would check ourselves over, the odd bruise or small cut was often found, but we used to laugh, run back up the hill and do it all over again, thankfully at that age we used to bounce fairly well so no lasting damage was done.

We did used to have to be a bit careful though as the area was the perfect habitat for Adders, Britain's only native poisonous snake, one occasion we were walking towards the spot we used to grass sledge when Dad just froze and pointed down towards his feet, there right where his next step would have gone was not one, but an entire nest of Adders, its the only time in my life I've seen so many Adders in one spot and still a vivid image in my mind as it was such a special thing to see, Dad carefully pulled his foot back and we watched as the snakes disappeared into the long grass.

Unfortunately the area we used to use for grass sledging has been taken over by Ash trees these days as mother nature marches on and the grass, although still there in patches the last time I went up there, is not there in sufficient quantity to make it viable for me to grab a sack and go grass sledging again, which is probably not a bad thing, as I don't bounce as well as I did when I was a boy.

When we got to the lower path we were in wonderland, surrounded by trees and plants, the foot paths lined with the huge leaves of the Burdock, the magnificent floral display of the Foxglove, at ground level you would find Bluebells and Primroses amongst other things such as the inevitable nettle patches, the forest floor was carpeted in Dogs Mercury and combined with the mixed greens of the canopy overhead gave you a feeling of absolute peace, with the serenity only being disturbed by the tapping of a Woodpecker or the anguished flutter of a Wood Pigeon getting out of the way of these two legged interlopers.

The Dogs Mercury did make it very easy to spot the animal trails that would wind themselves through the woods and under and over logs and fallen trees, we didn't often follow them back then, but when I returned as an adult years later I did and still do love to follow these trails, although the Dogs Mercury is no longer there in the abundance it was, the trails are still easy to spot and follow and with a little bit of investigation and a keen eye you can even work out what animal made or was using the trails by following the tracks and sign they have left as they move through the forest, from the easy ones like Deer slots, to Badger & Fox prints, sometimes you don't even need your eyes to follow these signs of animal activity as your other senses like your sense of smell, will work for you, as they did for me on one tracking trip I made there a few years ago, I was following a trail which led me right into the middle of a Badger latrine, its not a pleasant place.

Of course tracking the animals here was not always limited to ground based activity, we would often be walking around the path and Mum & Dad would point out a birds egg on the forest floor, normally it was a Pigeons egg, but its still a magical find, just by looking at the egg we could tell if it had hatched, been dislodged from the nest or been predated by another bird or animal, it also meant that we should look up and there more often than not, was the unmistakable tangled mess of a Pigeons nest built precariously in the branches of the tree.

On one trip round the lower horseshoe we could hear some unusual sounds off in the woods, Mum & Dad knew what it was, it was a load of kids trying to stalk us and not doing a very good job of it, they were shouting and goading us as brave kids do in a group of peers, so mum grabbed the catapult that Dad had made for me, a proper Dennis The Menace one it was too, forked stick, square elastic and a leather pouch, she picked up a few bits of loose chalk from the side of the path and fired them high in the air and into the woods in the general direction of the kids, strangely enough they soon disappeared and we didn't see or hear them again that day.

Of course a trip to the Horseshoe didn't mean just going for a walk, we would go "off trail" and into the trees where my Sister and I were allowed to explore, run free and play, but always within the sight and sound of our parents

We would climb trees and fall out of them, use the wild Clematis vines as Tarzan ropes and try and swing through the trees whilst doing the Tarzan yell, and it wasn't just us doing it, Mum & Dad did it too, a really good family afternoon out and a perfect way for us to use our excess energy up.

Each Autumn when we went to the Horseshoe we would take in the glorious change in colours and smell of the woods, a nice pleasant deep earthy smell now filled the woods, we still played on the Clematis and climbed trees, but now we were able to enjoy some seasonal treats in the form of Hazelnuts and the wonderfully tasty Beechnuts, Dad would show us where to find them and we would spend ages going through the leaf litter beneath the Beech Trees looking for the tell tale tri-sided nuts, we always used to find a few to nibble on and I still enjoy searching for them each Autumn whenever im in a Beech woodland.

My trips to the Horseshoe were not limited to going there with the family, when I was old enough, a school friend and I used to walk from home via the Horseshoe to my Nan's in Steyning, which is where Mum or Dad would collect us later that day.

My friend and I used to walk up to Steyning Bowl then up past the three cornered field to the Upper Horseshoe, we would then descend through the trees, normally on our backsides, and find a spot in the woods where we would stop for lunch and a drink.

Once at our spot we would get a small fire going, over which we would suspend a cooking pot made from an old baked bean tin that had a bail made from a bit of wire coat hanger or the like, we only ever used to use the pot to make nettle tea, which at the time I used to love and I remember it tasting like raw runner beans, these days I find it tastes awful and I cant stand it, I much prefer these days to cook up some nettles that I can then eat like spinach, the cooking water is either discarded or on rare occasions used as a vegetable stock in something like a risotto or vegetable stew.

With our drink of tea made, it was time to break out the tomato sandwiches and sit there for a few minutes having a bite to eat, it didn't take long though for us to get bored just sitting and start messing around climbing trees and swinging on the vines.

Sometimes we used to take some fresh food with us to cook over the fire and this normally meant making "Twisters", a recipe that Dad had passed down to me, as he used to do the same thing when he was lad, there were two types of twister, one comprised taking a fresh loaf of bread with you and ripping out the soft insides, making a dough with it then making some bread sausages and wrapping them around a stick and placing it over the fire to toast, the other way was a simple, flour, water and salt dough that we took with us premixed, this again was formed into long sausages and wrapped around a stick and placed over the fire until golden brown, as with all breads it was done when it sounded hollow when you tapped it with a finger.

It was only years later that I discovered you should really take all of the bark off the stick you are using to wrap the dough around as the bark can harbour bacteria and of course you don't know what a bird might have deposited on it before you got to it, still, it never did us any harm and as the old saying goes "you have to eat a bit of dirt before you die".

When I took my nephews to these very same woods many years later we did exactly the same and had a small fire, over which we had a cooking pot made from an old tin and we cooked twisters in exactly the same fashion, although it being modern times, we also used to take some hot dog sausages with us and if you were clever and used the right sized stick, you could slide the twister off complete and then put a hot dog into the hole left by the stick for a woodsy snack.

Back to my trip with my school friend though, when it was time to move on and get to Nan's we would extinguish the fire and once we were sure it was out we would cover it over and head down to the lower path, this is where if we were feeling adventurous, or stupid as I would call it now, we would leave the path and go to the old chalk quarry.

We had no ropes, helmets or safety equipment, it was unheard of back then and we couldn't afford it anyway, we would throw our bags over the edge and then climb down the chalk face to the bottom to retrieve them, how we never fell or seriously hurt ourselves I'll never know, but we did it more than once and got away with it.

From here we would walk down the road, head across the Cricket field and head towards Nan's where we were met with a cheery smile from Nan & Grandad, a glass of squash and more often than not a slice of home made cake, before getting in the car and heading home, tired but happy.

In later years I would take my nephews to these very same woods and do all the things that I used to do as a kid, swinging on the Tarzan ropes, making camps, cooking simple meals and sometimes just sitting there enjoying each others company, although unlike when I was a lad, we used to take small packable hammocks with us, so much more comfortable than the ground or a wet log to sit on.

One trip that my nephews and I took to The Horseshoe saw us sitting in our hammocks up in the woods, when down slope of us we heard the unmistakable sound of something moving through the woods, leaves rustled and twigs snapped, we wondered what it could be, it was big whatever it was.

We sat quiet and still and just watched, then out of the understorey two Roe Deer appeared, totally oblivious to our presence just a few tens of yards up the slope from them. We all sat motionless as these deer just meandered through the woods until they just melted away into the woods, moments like that are priceless.

Of course there is a lot more than Deer in the woods and one of the things I love to do now is to just go and sit quiet and see what comes to me, I've witnessed Deer, Squirrels, Foxes, Rabbits, Badgers, small rodents, Birds of Prey as well numerous species of smaller birds like Great Tits, Tree Creepers and the like, just by sitting nice and quiet and becoming accepted as part of the area by nature.

In recent years the woodland has been decimated by Ash die back disease, and although its very sad to see the trees die, Ash does form a monoculture with some areas looking like Bamboo plantations as the Ash saplings take over and crowd everything else out, however the vast open spaces that have been created in the woodland have allowed sunlight to penetrate to the forest floor once again and seeds of Bluebell, Primrose, Celandine, Spurge, Dogs Mercury and the ever present Nettles that have lain dormant for years have been exposed to the light and have all germinated and are now starting to spread and once again carpet the woodland floor.

The Estate though has the unenviable task and expense of making sure all of the public footpaths are safe for people to walk on, the last thing they or anybody wants is for someone to be hit by a branch falling off an infected Ash tree, the work they have done is incredible, but its not been to the liking of everyone and there have been some moans and groans from those that simply do not understand the situation and why this work is essential.

One upside from all of the felling that had to take place though, is that like the naturally exposed areas, sunlight is now penetrating to the forest floor alongside the paths and as above, seeds that have lain dormant for years are all springing into life and each Spring these paths are now a riot of colour and its quite funny that some of those that moaned, are now saying how pretty it looks, nothing stranger than folk I guess.

The Ash will naturally be replaced by other species such as Sycamore and Hazel and thankfully some Ash trees are showing a natural resistance to the fungus that is attacking them, so not all is lost and hopefully the open spaces that have been created will allow a few of the dormant Beech nuts that the Squirrels have not gotten to, to germinate and continue the long standing tradition of these majestic trees growing on these hallowed slopes.

Secret Spot

Another favourite place of ours to visit was a place we commonly called the Secret Spot, its a place located within walking distance of our normal haunts, but being just a little further out it was very rarely if ever visited by anyone else and the chances of anyone finding this particular spot in the woods in reality was pretty remote, again it was a place that Dad knew well from his childhood and that he wanted to share with us.

I used to love going up there, but on little legs it was quite a hike, so we travelled fairly light, either that or Dad was the donkey with everything in a rucksack on his back, I cant really remember which, but have an inkling both statements are probably true.

We would park the car at the top end of a small lane that had very little traffic and would then walk over the fields towards the big house, once at the wall for the big house we turned left and started the trek uphill to our spot.

On the way up we passed the old hay barn, which still stands, shortly afterwards we were in the woods and took a path that was most probably an old droveway in years past, this path was now the approach to our wonderland.

The path had been travelled by man and beast for hundreds if not thousands of years, something that could and can be attested by the fact that it has been eroded so much by years and years of footfall, that it now sits well below the surrounding ground levels in it's own deep cut in the hillside.

With the sides of the path now towering above us on each side, we would continue up the path ducking under the odd tree that had fallen across the gulley we were travelling in, forming natural bridges for the wildlife between the sides of this man made valley, approaching the top of the path we approach the spot where we leave the relatively safe surface of the path and head into the bush, pushing through the undergrowth, bramble and briar's until we burst into a grassy glade in the middle of the woods, this was our secret spot and it always felt good to eventually get there.

The glade itself was carpeted with short neatly mown grass thanks to the local rabbit population, although the beautifully manicured surface was also populated with some very large ant hills, but despite these there was plenty of room to run around and if you went there at just the right time of year, there was always a magnificent harvest of wild strawberries, which despite their small size, knock commercially grown berries into a cocked hat, there is nothing that can beat the burst of flavour that a wild strawberry gives, later in the year the secret spot gave up another delicacy with a bountiful harvest of Beech nuts that had fallen from the huge Beech trees that grew up here.

The mighty Beech's that grew here were amazing things to play on and around, with one of them being an easy climbing tree, as one limb many years ago had arched down to the ground where it now rested, as if it was a huge arm reaching down from the tree that had its elbow resting on the ground and its forearm raising back up again, this limb was so wide that we would walk up it to the main trunk of the tree then carefully come back down, it was always a great plaything, this tree is still there, but these days is a sad reflection of its former self as it has reached the end of its life and is now little more than a rotting stump, a great shame, but all good things do come to an end after all.

The glade however big enough that we could play tennis in it and we would often take the swingball rackets with us and have a play around, just remembering that there were ant hills around to trip you up and trip you up they did, we have a great photograph of Mum in full flight backwards as she fell over one of these hills.

The glade although open was of course flanked by the woods, with the big Beech tree on one side, open woodland to the east and the northern side being full of small, but flexible Ash saplings of perhaps eight to twelve feet or so high, one trick that Dad showed us fairly early on in our trips to the secret spot was how to climb up these saplings until you could go no further, then start to sway.

The continual swaying slowly built up momentum until you were rocking back and forth like a pendulum on a clock, eventually you built up enough movement and through the swaying had softened up the base of the sapling that it bent all the way over and you ended up at the top of the tree, still holding on but laying on your back on the ground, where you promptly let go of the Sapling and it returned to its normal vertical aspect with a great whoosh as the leaves and branches parted the air on its journey back to normality.

Dad decided he would have a go at this on one trip up there, so he shinned up a suitable looking tree and got a good distance up and started swaying and trying to build up that all important momentum, unfortunately it was a bit too early in the year and the sap had not risen up the tree enough, so instead of swaying back and forth, the tree snapped about half way up with an almighty crack and deposited Dad firmly on his backside on the ground.

We used to build the odd camp up here too, but not that often as there was always so much else to do, it was always a shame to leave the secret spot and head home, we always went home from here tired, but very happy.

I visited the secret spot again many years later and the grassy glade was gone, the ant hills were no more and the big old Beech tree as mentioned was nothing more than a rotting stump, the ground is now just chalk and flint with a sparse covering of Dogs Mercury and most of the area has been taken over by Ash & Sycamore trees, some places now resemble Bamboo plantations as the Ash saplings grow so thickly that it is nigh on impossible to walk through them and it is clearly evident that more people come up here than they ever used to with unofficial mountain bike trails and jumps cut into the woodland floor.

Despite the "influx" of people up here now it is still possible to go there, sling up a hammock and sit nice and quiet in the woods without seeing anybody all day, just you, a brew and nature, its also the spot where I saw my most unusual bit of wildlife, I was sitting quiet in my hammock just taking it all in, when behind me I heard a rustle in the leaf litter, I turned around and to my amazement there was a Peacock in its full glory, it was totally unfussed that I was there and just kept walking and pecking at the ground as it made its way past me, I can only assume it came out of the big house and so was used to people, then despite its amazing colours and long tail dragging behind it, it just vanished into the woodland and I never saw it again.

Two lasting memories of more recent trips to the Secret Spot are firstly where after many attempts, I finally managed to make fire by friction, i.e. rubbing two sticks together and I can still remember the feeling of elation as I looked down at the pile of smouldering dust I had created, despite common misconception, rubbing two sticks together does not create a flame, just an ember, but I had done it and done it at one of the favourite spots from my childhood, pure magic.

The other memory is on a trip up there with two friends, one of whom I was going to play a bit of a prank on, to this end I had a small bag of black olives with me that I had stashed in my pocket. Upon arrival at the spot where we would be spending our day, I made the excuse of going for an explore, so off I trundled, taking my time and looking at whatever I could find as I normally did, they were both used to me going off on a wander like this, so nothing looked out of place or unusual, I must say that it was also up here that I had my best find ever, when I found a Fallow Deer antler that was just laying on the ground, I still have that antler in my workshop as a reminder of good times.

As I walked around I found a suitable looking spot on the ground that had some nice moss on it that the olives would contrast against beautifully, so I stooped down and deposited two of the black fruits from my pocket, then called my friends over to look at this amazing find.

Over they came, one clocked the ruse straight away and thankfully played along with it, not that I hadn't let him on it on the way here of course, he exclaimed *"look at the size of these droppings!"*, I acknowledged his comment and stated that they must have been from a Fallow Deer as they were quite large and I said they also look fairly fresh, the other guy wasn't overly interested, but did comment when I stooped down once more and proceeded to pick one up and start mauling it between my fingers *"urgh, that's horrible, put it down, you don't know where its been"*, my mate who was in on the joke commented *"we know exactly where it's been"* and laughed.

I studied the dropping with some interest and said *"it has to from a Fallow Deer"* I went on to say there was one sure fire test to see if it was from a Fallow Deer and that was to do a Bear Grylls on it, and do an oral scat exam, i.e. – eat it!

The older chap nearly threw up as I put this *"dropping"* into my mouth and started to chew, *"ummm, definitely a Fallow Deer"* I said.

His face was an absolute picture when I then swallowed this dropping down and my other friend said *"prove its gone, open your mouth so we can see"*, so that's what I did and of course it was all gone, the guys face was a perfect mix of horror and disbelief at what I had done.

I was of course laughing like a thing possessed inside and to this day, I don't think the other chap ever cottoned on to the joke that was being played that day.

The Targets

The Targets are as the name suggests a set of shooting targets that are located at the head of a very steep sided valley at the base of the South Downs.

The Targets were first used back in the mid to late 1800's, although most if not all of the remaining infrastructure that you can see there now, dates back to the second world war.

We didn't visit the targets as a venue such that much when I was younger, more often than not just passing through them on our way somewhere else, like the Beeches or as an alternative route to The Lump, but I do remember the targets being in use and live firing taking place, often walking along the top of the hill and seeing the red "Live Firing" flags flying, not that you couldn't hear them shooting of course.

Dad could remember the Targets being used by the Canadians for live fire practice back in WW2 and he would reminisce about the times he and his friends would collect the live .303 rounds that the soldiers had dropped around the place and how these rounds would be deposited in an old hollow tree stump that sat at the head of the springs in the valley bottom.

Once the rounds had been deposited Dad and his friends would light a fire on top of the pile of live brass and lead and then run like hell before the rounds cooked in the heat and went off with an almighty bang, that because of the nature of the time, nobody batted an eyelid at, they were used to pops and bangs from the valley, so people thought nothing of it.

My memories of the targets are nowhere near as explosive, but are filled with some drama.

One winter we took our sledge to the top of the southern side of the targets as it had snowed quite heavily and this side of the targets being in shade all day was frozen solid. So having had a few gentle runs on the top, I was encouraged by Mum & Dad to go a bit further down, but rather than sit on the sledge it was "suggested" that I lay down on it and go head first, so that's what I did and of course trusting my parents, I believed them when they said *"its not that steep!"*.

So laying head first on the sledge, I was given a gentle push and off I went, trundling nice and smoothly down the gentle slope, that's when all hell broke loose, as I picked up speed I approached the true edge of the valley side and as I disappeared from the sight of my parents on the top of the hill, im now not on a gentle slope, but what felt like a near vertical slope, they told me later, much to their amusement, that as I went over the edge all they heard was a scream.

Travelling at considerable speed down the valley side, im now jumping rabbit warrens and smashing through old thistle stalks, then I get to the bottom where you might think I was able to slow down nice and easily and make a return to the top of the valley, oh no, I hadn't put two and two together when we first got there, the north slope being in full sunshine was not covered in snow as the sun had melted it.

As I approached the valley floor at Mach 2, I noticed that the snow and ice I was travelling on ended in a very neat line right up the middle of the valley floor, basically anything that was in the shadow of the southern side was snow and ice, anything that had even a drop of sunshine on it was slush, mud and pain.

I got to the defining line and this is where my journey stopped, well, the sledge stopped on a sixpence as it buried itself in the soft ground, I on the other hand carried on with my journey, slid off the sledge and over I went, sky, mud, sky, mud and so it went on until I had stopped tumbling and came to a halt.

Picking myself up off the valley floor, thankfully no broken bones, I got myself together, walked back to where my sledge had come to a halt and removed it from the mud and slowly climbed back to the top of the slope, where I was met by Mum, Dad & Sister in absolute hysterics, I was asked if I wanted another go - erm, no thanks.

I still go to the targets but normally just walk through on my way through to another area, much the same as we used to in years previous, the sides of the valley do however appear to be very much steeper than they ever used to be, the old tree

Dad used to blow up is long gone, but the springs are still there, as are the actual target mechanisms.

You can still go and explore the targets and the apparatus that made them work and much to the credit of the Estate (Steyning Downland Scheme) along with their band of faithful and hard working volunteers, have tided up the area and have restored one of the targets to full working use, although they do not and have no future plans to allow shooting here again, it is a credit to them to restore the area so current and indeed future generations can view and understand the importance and history of the area.

In recent years the ecological management of the area has been taken over by SDS and through the hard work of SDS staff and volunteers the area has been transformed into a wildlife oasis, with a major feather in their cap being the recolonisation of the area by the rare Duke of Burgundy butterfly.

Bunnyland

Bunnyland, not its proper name but the name given to this area by the locals, it gets its name as you might imagine due to the once huge population of rabbits that used to call it home.

Our trips to Bunnyland were once or twice a year and for one reason – Blackberrying.

Bunnyland sits on the South Downs within walking distance from home, but its far to steep to farm, so for generations it had been left to go wild and not only housed many hundreds of rabbits, but also deep, thick, luscious bramble bushes that held the most spectacular blackberries and very few people knew about it or indeed had the permission to go up there, as schemes such as open access didn't exist and this was well off the public footpath and bridleways.

Armed with baskets, walking sticks and a packet of plasters for the inevitable injuries you get from the bramble we would set off to Bunnyland for an afternoons fruit picking, my Sister and I more often than not ate more berries than we saved to take home with us and certainly got no sympathy if we later complained of having a stomach ache, we would get told, *"well you were warned and its your own fault"*, I don't think we ever did learn that lesson, the big, fat juicy berries were just too much of a temptation.

Needless to say, we didn't spend all of our time just picking blackberries, we would also just sit and look out over the valley below and what a commanding view it was too, across the valley on the opposing slope was what I now know as my sit tree, the entire area was a place of great adventure, with very steep sides that made even the fittest puff like mad by the time they got to the top, we would get scratched to bits just trying to get up to where our bounty lay, let alone all the stabbings we would get from the thorns as we harvested the fruits.

I had a friend who used to live in one of the farm cottages at the foot of Bunnyland and we would go to his house in school summer holidays and would soon be off out and through the farmyard, whilst his and my mum had a cuppa and a chin wag, if I remember correctly he had a younger sister which was handy as it meant my Sister could play with her whilst we boys went exploring.

We would go across the fields and into the old chalk quarry that had been burrowed into the side of the hill, then one day they were gone, I never did find out what happened to them or where they went, it was a real shame as it selfishly meant one less area to go and explore.

I do still walk around Bunnyland which is now under the stewardship of a different farmer who has put some of his land under the Open Access scheme thereby enabling people to take a walk away from the footpath and go and explore the area, now after many years im able to get back to the Yew wood I used to play in as a child and can fully explore and appreciate some of the more open areas that are almost park like with their large trees dotted around like small islands in a sea of grass.

Sitting there under a tree using its trunk against my back as a backrest is one of my favourite things to do and its quite amazing what can be seen for those who are willing to invest a little time just sitting quiet with Deer, Badgers, Foxes and Rabbits making an appearance, with Buzzards circling overhead, Kestrels hovering on the gentle breeze and more recently the amazing aerobatic antics of the Red Kites which are slowly making a comeback.

Just occasionally you might get a herd of cattle around you, but they are just being inquisitive and as long as you don't do anything stupid like getting in between a mother and her calf, you'll be fine.

<u>The Lump</u>

The Lump was a special place for the entire family when we were growing up and its a place we used to frequent at all times of the year, located high up on the South Downs with commanding views over Steyning and the Brooks, we could see for miles over the Weald and along the line of the Downs to the east towards Brighton & Devils Dyke.

From this position high up on the hill we would spend time trying to locate familiar places in the town below, the Cricket Field, St Andrews Church and Nan & Grandad's house where we would end up later for tea, squash and Nan's home made cake and depending on the time of year, a raid on Grandad's garden and the Blackcurrant and Strawberry patches, being ever so careful not to knock his prize Chrysanthemums as we piled in.

As stated above we used to visit the lump at all times of the year, in the winter the view from here was amazing, all the leaves on the trees had fallen giving a much better view of our surroundings, the Weald had that desolate, cold, but nevertheless, beautiful look to it, you could see wisps of smoke rising from chimneys as the residents did their best to keep warm and looking out over the Brooks, which each winter turned into a a huge lake as they always flooded in the winter following the winter rains, Mum & Dad used to tell us about how when they were younger they would go ice skating on the Brooks and how much fun they used to have, we unfortunately never got to experience this though.

Back to the lump, the base of which marked the starting point for the most incredible sledge run, that was nice and gentle for a change and not the death slide I experienced in the targets.

Starting at the base of the lump you had more or less a dead straight run all the way down the path to the bottom of the field, right to the junction where the path from the lower horseshoe joins and if you got spot on you could carry on all the way down the path to the allotments, although this long run was usually reserved until we were leaving, as the walk back up was exhausting.

On one occasion when I had completed a sledge run which had ended in an abrupt stop as I lost control and tumbled down the hill for a few yards, I found myself covered in claret, a quick examination saw that I had somehow cut my wrist open on something.

Following the sledge tracks and the red dots that contrasted against the whiteness of the snow, soon revealed the culprit that had caused my injury, a small stump from a very small

Ash sapling was nestled down in the snow, it's top at an acute angle where it had been nibbled by an animal, but it was protruding just enough that I had caught my wrist on it on the way down, I hadn't felt a thing as it sliced me open, I still have the scar from that escapade on my right wrist as a reminder of those times.

Springtime visits were always a pleasure, Mum & Dad pointing out all of the fresh new growth following the bleak winter months, the trees springing back to life with fresh green buds and leaves, the Cowslips lining the path on the sunny south facing slopes, their mass of blooms contrasting with the dainty Primroses single flowers peeking out from the woodland edge.

Climbing to the top of the lump we would sit for a while and get our breath back and have a drink, it wasn't long before my Sister and I were off running around again, Mum & Dad would sit and relax in the spring sunshine and recharge their batteries, Dad worked some very long hours back then and Mum, well she had me and my Sister to look after, as well as running the house, shopping & cooking dinner for us all.

Whilst they sat in the sunshine we were left to run around, climb trees and explore the immediate area, just occasionally we would get a shout from Mum or Dad as we got a bit boisterous and/or had drifted just that little bit too far away, we would soon settle back down and drift back towards them.

Dad would point out the birds around us busy building their nests or flitting around with beaks full of insects to feed their already hatched young.

As we sat there we would undertake our normal game of spotting places down below us in the town, the church, cricket field were east to spot, but we would be tasked with finding more obscure places that we knew, but from up here looked so very different, looking out over the Brooks we could see the grassy fields that now laid where just a few weeks previous there was a lake, the only water now being the many streams and the silver ribbon of the River Adur dissecting the floodplain.

The Brooks were a place we didn't visit that often, but I'll briefly digress from being at the Lump and we will take a brief diversion to the Brooks where I can recall one trip where we were walking over the brooks, jumping the small streams and just seeing what we could see in this very different environment to what we used to.

As we walked along through the long grasses that framed the streams so beautifully, out of nowhere a Hare up and bolted, I jumped out of my skin as I hadn't seen it in the long grass and had nearly stepped on it, we watched it disappear over the field, then Dad told me to put my hand where the Hare had been sitting, I couldn't believe how warm the ground was, sorry for disturbing you Mr Hare.

On one other trip over there we didn't see any Hare's but we did get charged by a herd of cattle, now the worst thing you can do is run, so Dad just stopped in his tracks, turned around and shouted "BOO" at the top of his voice, the cattle stopped dead in their tracks, almost comically as they put their front legs out in front of them like something out of a Saturday morning cartoon, but they had stopped and an important lesson was learnt that day of what to and what not to do if you get charged by cattle.

Back to the lump and its time for a summer trip, with the sun beating down hard on our backs the walk up to the lump is much harder than usual due to the heat, the lush green grasses of springtime are making way to the parched browns of a long, hot summer and we are on the lookout for Adders, I don't really recall seeing that many here, perhaps just the tail end of one or two as they slid gracefully away from us as we approached.

What we can see however is the evidence of the Rabbit population, lots of short grass alongside the woodland edge where the bunnies have been grazing, on top of the abundant ant hills we see evidence of the Foxes being around marking their territories by leaving their scat on a high point for other Foxes to see, and smell.

Just occasionally we find an owl pellet, which dad carefully prises apart to reveal the bones of its prey, I would wonder at the number of small bones, jaws and skulls that are revealed, not only indicating the owls prey, but also the general health of the area, as studying the pellets will show the species of mammals being preyed upon such as mice and voles, studying owl pellets is still something I find fascinating and I continue to break them apart to this day to see what bounty lays inside.

Of course natures bounty abounds for us humans too, with wild Strawberries lurking in the grass, Salad Burnett grows tight to the ground so as to avoid being a rabbits next meal, but we can pick a few pieces and a quick nibble awakens the taste buds with a glorious cucumber flavour, the brambles and Dog Rose are in flower indicating the harvest to come later in the year, a quick look at the Blackthorn & Hawthorn bushes shows small fruits already starting to grow and if you know where to look, there is a solitary Crab Apple that's laden with hundreds of small burgeoning fruits that make the most amazing apple sauce later in the year.

Summer at the lump was more about just chilling out, it was quite often far too hot and sweaty after the walk up to go running around, so our time there was more like a pit stop before we headed off into the woods and some welcome shade on a round robin walk that took us over to the Beeches and the old barn, before heading back down hill past the old orchard and invariably then to Nan's for tea & cake.

Autumn was a time of plenty, the Blackberries were in season and we used to pick a few to eat and some to take home, ok a lot to eat and a few to take home for Blackberry & Apple crumble as afters to tonight's dinner, the Haws, Sloes & Crab Apples were not quite ready, not that it ever stopped us trying them, we would be given some Sloes to eat and having been told they were delicious we would just pop them into our mouths and chew, Mum and Dad would laugh at our reactions, as the sourness hit and our faces screwed up in reaction to the fruits, of course when I took my nephews up there many years later, I would do exactly the same thing to them and laugh at their reaction and I hope that in years to come they will do the same with their children, thereby following a bit of a tradition of sorts.

The autumn is a time of colour and the leaves of the Sycamores have taken on their magnificent autumnal colours of yellow, golds and deep reds and russets, the Ash & Hazel were all going yellow as the life giving sap withdrew from their previously luscious leaves, there were a few Hazelnuts around, but not many as we never seemed to beat the Squirrels to them up here, the Ash keys were hanging off the soon to be bare branches of the Ash trees like huge clumps of Spanish Moss that you see in pictures of the swamps in the southern United States.

There were a few treats though, a forage beneath the old Beech tree would provide a handful of Beechnuts to nibble on and the fungi and mushrooms were everywhere, we never picked any though as the opportunity to make a mistake, sometimes a deadly one, was always there, the old adage of *"if in doubt, leave it out"* was a good one and one we stuck to, Mum & Dad knew a few mushroom varieties, but we always stayed away just in case inquisitive little minds and hands picked the wrong one.

Before long we have gone full circle and its wintertime again and I hope it snows so we can get the sledge out, no injuries this year though if we can help it.

Coming up to the modern day and I still visit the lump on a regular basis, the view of old is now obscured in some directions by the masses of Ash saplings that have taken over and that grow unhindered as they are no longer cut down by the Rabbits thanks to myxomatosis that decimated the Rabbit population and with these ever hungry lawn mowers gone, the Ash saplings have thrived, the once grassy slopes replaced by a thick monoculture of trees, with bare earth and a canopy that the sun struggles to penetrate.

All is not lost however, as the Estate had a project under way to fell many of these small Ash trees that have grown here in an effort to restore the open grassland and it seems to be working as the slope that leads to the lump was cleared a couple years ago and once the sunlight could get to the ground the area regenerated very quickly, the grass has regrown, the wild flowers are back and all the hard work paid off.

Little did anyone know however that nature had a sting in its tail and was going to offer a way to clear the Ash without human intervention when Ash Die Back disease hit and what a devastating effect it would have on our native Ash trees, now the clearance jobs are not to clear Ash to restore habitat, but to clear the tons and tons of dead Ash that now poises a safety issue.

Nature will prevail though as she always does as some Ash trees appear to be resistant to the fungus and those areas that have been laid bare up by The Lump, much like those in the Horseshoe, will soon be taken over by pioneer species such as Sycamore and in time return the area to the way I remember it when I was a mere nipper.

Evening Shoot

I was always an occasional shooter and I ever only shot for the pot, never for sport, I was bought up to follow the very simple rule of a one shot, one kill, if you were in anyway unsure of making a clean kill, you didn't even consider taking the shot.

One of the best nights shooting I ever had though was conveniently located right at the bottom of the garden, this particular permission is a horse field that adjoins our property.

The landowner at the time had a bit of a problem with rabbits digging up the field and having horses out there the last thing he wanted was for a horse to step in a rabbit hole and hurt itself, so after speaking with him one afternoon, permission to shoot was sought and granted.

The field is not overly large, just a few acres, but the abundance of wildlife out there is incredible, Rabbits, Pheasants, Badgers, Foxes, birds of prey, summer and winter migrant birds, such as the Black Redstart, as well as hoards of our native bird life, not too mention the masses of Butterflies, Moths and numerous other insects and spiders.

The field is surrounded by Hawthorn, Blackthorn and Elder trees and at one end of the field are a dozen or so free standing Hawthorn trees in the field itself that give the horses some summer shade and a barrier against the winter wind and rain, these trees also happen to be my favourite spot to locate for an evenings shooting, as they gave me cover and shade too.

Each year the field would be closed off to the horses so the grass could grow with a view to strip grazing it later in the year and it was only when the field was closed, that I considered going out there for a shoot as it meant that there was no danger whatsoever of a horse wandering into my field of fire, nor would I have the unpleasant experience of a horse creeping up on me unheard and me then spooking it, the last thing I wanted was hundreds of pounds of Cobb getting the wind up it with me in close proximity, therefore by choice, I only went out there when the field was shut.

With the field being closed to grazing, of course everything grew like mad and it was soon looking akin to a wild flower meadow of old, lots of tall grasses, Clover and Field Bind Weed with its delicate pink and white trumpet shaped flowers, but also to those with a keen eye species such as Black Meddick, Ragged Robin, Vetches & Trefoil grew, along with taller species like Fat Hen and Nettles growing in clumps around the field, giving away the secret past as they typically grew on the sites of the old farm buildings that are long gone, but whose lumps and bumps of their stony remains can still be seen, the nettles in particular growing in areas of high nitrates betraying the past when livestock was kept and stabled here, there are also areas that show the scars of more recent times, in particular the old bomb crater from WW2 that lays towards the western end of the field.

Back to my best nights shooting, this one evening will stay with me forever, although it is my best ever nights shooting, I never actually took a shot.

I had been at work all day up in the woods enjoying the dappled sunshine and gentle breeze that filtered through the woods high up on the South Downs, returning home and the heat of the day was subsiding into one of those glorious early summer evenings, the breeze had subsided to a mere whisper and it was simply – pleasant.

Sitting on the patio I looked out over the field watching the butterflies flitting around looking for somewhere to roost for the night, but I could also see a number of Rabbits, so seeing an opportunity to get one for the pot, I went and got changed into my shooting gear, grabbed my air rifle and popped over the garden wall, being careful to avoid the electric fence (which I had experienced a belt from more than once) and into the field.

I decided my best option was to go and settle in amongst the Hawthorns at the end of the field and wait for the bunnies to come to me, I walked slowly and cautiously through the long grass watching hundreds of Grasshoppers jumping out of the way as I disturbed them, as I approached the trees the grasses thinned out and the level of disturbance to the insects around me was drastically reduced, it was already a good evening and I hadn't even taken the gun out of its case yet.

After a short while I was nearing my favourite spot, a nice area with a sturdy tree behind me that I could lean against for comfort and also to disguise my shape, in front of me the ground rose towards the south giving me a perfect backstop that would stop any pellet in its tracks, I could see plenty of evidence of the Rabbits feeding in this area, the grass had been nibbled low and tight and the tell tale Rabbit poops were everywhere.

As I settled beneath the tree and with the last rays of the sun slowly bathing the hedge line in its wondrous orange glow and what little wind there was gently occasionally moving the tops of the tall grass, I was set, all I needed were a few bunnies to show.

I sat and waited taking in my surroundings,but ready to pounce when the opportunity presented itself, overhead the occasional Bat flew over, wonderful to see and a real summer treat, the Pigeons were all leaving the trees around and flying off towards their night time roosts in the Copse, a lone Buzzard was receiving its last heckling of the day from the local Crow population before that all too found somewhere to settle for the upcoming night.

Suddenly to my left a movement, was it bunny, nope it was better as the Vixen appeared out of nowhere, now I knew there was an Earth in the corner of the field, had been for years, but I had not seen the Foxes for some time, I now had competition for the bunnies!

She cautiously moved out of the hedge, then much to my surprise, three cubs followed her out, absolutely amazing, as I sat there in the shadow of the Hawthorn, I knew the Vixen had not seen or even sensed my presence, for if she had, she would have been long gone.

The Vixen and her offspring slowly moved out into the open, noses down searching for food, the cubs though were not having much of it for long and were soon chasing each other and running around as kids of all species do.

They all slowly drew nearer, but became more cautious as they came ever closer to the long grass, they still hadn't seen me, the cubs disposition changed as they got deeper into the long grass, no longer playing, but exploring, searching and sniffing out that next meal, all three of them perfect miniatures of their mother.

Still closer they came, my heart started to pound, surely they would see me soon?

Closer they come, sniffing around the bottoms of the trees, but I can now only see two cubs, where is the third?, I cant see it anywhere, then out of the corner of my eye I see the third cub, its a brave little soul, all on its own and less than five or six meters away from me, I don't dare to breathe less the sound or movement of my chest spooks it, still closer it comes, now less than three meters away from me.

I'm paralysed, please nose don't itch, im now almost too scared to move my eyes let alone anything else as the cub sits down, looks straight at me with those inquisitive eyes, but it doesn't flinch, either its fearless or it really hasn't sensed me.

A bead of sweat bubbles up from my temple and runs down the side of my face, my heart is thumping so hard it could be used as a hammer, the cub stands, still not aware that im there, it turns and heads back along the path it followed when it first appeared by my side, then it stops, hunches down on all fours with its stare fixated on something, perhaps its prey, but no, its waiting in ambush for its siblings who are just out of range of its pounce, as they approach the cub springs forward in an explosion of grass pollen, fur and muscle to mock attack its brothers or sisters, all three end up in a tumble of fur in the long grass before one makes a break for it and runs off towards to open field, soon being followed by the other two, all three run down the field where they join the Vixen.

Off course by now all of the bunnies are long gone back to the safety of their burrows, can you blame them?, but nor do I care, what an absolutely awe inspiring few minutes and as stated earlier, one that will remain with me for as long as I live, you simply cannot put a price or value on that type of experience.

Now the Foxes have disappeared I can at last move my body, still tense from my temporary paralysis, as I relax and start to breathe again my heart rate drops and it now longer feels like a power hammer in my chest, as the calmness returns im filled with a sense of euphoria that no drug could emulate.

Time is getting on now, its very nearly dark and I need a cup of tea, I slowly extract myself from my spot beneath the Hawthorn, I empty my gun into the ground and put it back in its case and head home through the long grass that now seems to be devoid of those Grasshoppers.

Shortly after this magical evening,it was very noticeable that the Rabbit population in the field had plummeted, but there were three rather plump Fox cubs and their mother out in the field, did I mind the competition, not at all, I would gladly trade every evening out there to recreate that experience once more.

One Last Cast

With Dad having such a stressful job, one of his releases was fishing, its an ideal way to unwind and forget all of your financial, personal and work worries, they just seem to melt away for a few hours, its just you, your thoughts and nature.

So quite often in the summer when the long evenings gave a respite from the heat of the day, meteorological or otherwise, Dad would come home from work, get changed and we would all go down to the beach as a family for a couple of hours, we would go to Goring if the tide was out so we could go rock pooling or push our shrimping nets through the shallows, then sit there by the waters edge sorting out our catch, the shrimp going into a bucket to be cooked up at home for the freshest, tastiest shrimp salads you ever had, the small fish and crabs we used to get were all returned to the sea.

If the tide was in, we went to Shoreham for a swim, although we always took a rod or two and some Mackerel feathers with us, just in case we were lucky enough to snag a few Mackerel for the pot, sometimes we hit the jackpot though as the shoals of Mackerel made the sea literally boil as they were attacked by predatory fish such as Bass and when the Mackerel were really on it, we could be found running up and the down the beach following the shoal, quite often the problem was knowing when to stop, although Mackerel are delicious, there really are only so many you can eat or freeze for the future.

Of course my fishing was not limited to going with the family and when I was old enough to go on my own – I did, and as often as I could.

Thankfully one of my school friends lived just up the road and he was as mad about fishing as I was, so we spent many an hour in our school holidays travelling down to the beach at low tide on our push bikes, garden fork strapped to the cross bar (tines facing backwards I hasten to add) and a bucket suspended from the handles to go and dig some bait, coming home a few hours later to sort out our gear ready for the next day when we would cycle to the harbour arm at Shoreham or down to Worthing Pier.

We both enjoyed our fishing a great deal, but being a couple of lads there was also a fair amount of fooling around too, with dares like who would eat a Lugworm sandwich or letting a Rag Worm pinch the tip of your tongue with its pincers to seeing who could cast the furthest amongst other things.

One trip that my friend and I made to Worthing Pier, saw us set up on the old cast iron landing stage right at the very end of the pier, I was on the eastern side facing towards Brighton and had cast out my baits and was patiently waiting for a bite.

We were joined on this trip by a lad I didn't know, but whom was a friend of my mate, he was a nice enough chap, but took his fishing very seriously and as my friend and I got bored waiting for a bite we started to mess around, unbeknown to me this other lad had seen a clonking great bite on my rod and seeing that I was nowhere close had struck into the bite before yelling down to me and telling me I had a fish on.

As I reeled in I could feel some weight on the end, then as it surfaced I was presented with the biggest Plaice I had ever caught, it was huge and I would have missed it entirely if it were not for the other chap being there.

Fast forward 35 years or so to the present day and to when I was recently in hospital, a new chap arrived on the ward I was in and went into the bed opposite mine, over the following days we got chatting and found we both had fishing in common, he told me his story and I told him mine from the time I was in the Queens Head Club in Brighton to the present day, when I mentioned the Queens Head his ears pricked up as he exclaimed that he also used to fish for the Queens Head Club.

With some serious common ground we chatted for hours about the "old days" and how my friend and I were two of a small handful of juniors in the club at the time and how I was close to winning the Junior Cup one year, he told me his son was also a junior in that club and it must have been around the same time I was there.

We carried on chatting and he asked what my friends name was, so I told him, you could have knocked him out of his chair, not only did he know my friend, but he still fished with his Dad to this day, we then worked out that the lad who had hooked that large Plaice I didn't know about, was his son!

Later that week his son came to see his Dad, so the story was recounted to him, he remembers fishing off the Pier, he knew and still does know my old friend who I lost contact with many years ago, but he couldn't remember that particular trip to the Pier, talk about a small world.

We didn't just go to the beach, some trips were made with a group of friends to a small stream a few miles from home, the stream was not only picturesque, but it was deep and we had spotted a few fish swimming around in it, mainly Roach & Rudd but they were biggies.

Of course the stream was on private land, but we didn't let that bother us, I know the landowner could see us, but all the time we behaved and left things alone we were fine, although we did get turfed off a couple of times, we used to go to this idyllic spot a couple of times each school summer holiday, armed with very basic coarse fishing tackle, a few garden worms and a loaf of bread for bait.

We would spread ourselves out along the crystal clear stream, nestling ourselves down in amongst the reeds and tall grass that fringed the stream, where we would bait up and drop the tackle into the water, no need to cast here as it was so narrow, we would each sit there in our own spot, enjoying the summer sun in proper "Swallows and Amazons" style, waiting patiently for our quarry to arrive, there was no guess work involved as you could see the shoals of fish swim up and down the stream, but would that big Roach we all wanted be there and would it take that very tasty looking piece of bread that was so clearly visible.

When the fish arrived our hearts would thump as the fish inspected the bait, then the fish would mouth the bait before swallowing it down, boom, quick strike to set the hook and the fish is on, seconds later a pristine bar of silver is in the net, its a beautiful fish and to us a real monster Roach, at best no more than half a pound in weight, but its been caught, probably for the first time in its life.

The fish is carefully unhooked and admired for a few seconds before being gently returned to the water, where in a flash of brilliant silver as the sunlight reflects off its scales, it's gone.

This was a scenario that we would repeat a couple of times during the day, we were never going to catch huge amounts of fish here, but to us it was a magical place, far enough away from home to be on our own, wild enough to make an adventure of it, but close enough to home – just in case.

It didn't matter that sometimes we didn't even get a bite, just being there was enough, out in the countryside, surrounded by natural beauty, with Dragon & Damsel flies flitting around, Water Boatmen and Pond Skaters on the surface of the stream and all manner of Butterflies in the meadow behind us with Skylarks overhead, what more could you want, well perhaps a few more fish would have been nice.

Many years later I had the opportunity to visit the stream once more as I was doing some work for the landowner, this time though we went to the stream by 4x4 rather than on push bikes, the place had hardly changed, the water was till as crystal clear as I remembered it, although the bank side vegetation had encroached somewhat, and the stream didn't seem to be as wide as I remembered it, I even found my old favourite spot just up from the bend, I stood there for a few minutes just taking it all in, I didn't see any Roach or Rudd this time though, but I bet they are still there and just as pristine as they always used to be.

One trip we used to make as a family on an occasional basis, but one that has always stuck out in my mind, is when we used to travel light and go the East Harbour Arm at Shoreham.

Parking the car in Southwick, Mum, Dad, Sister and I would start the long trek over to the arm via the lock gates in the docks, then after safely negotiating them and looking in amazement at the size of the ships in the harbour we would head off towards the arm, it was quite a trek, especially for those of us with little legs, but the trip was nearly always worth it.

We were not after monsters, quite the opposite, we were going Smelt bashing!, Smelt for those who do not know the species are a small sea fish that never gets any bigger than a few ounces in weight, but they are a pretty fish and have an unusual smell, they smell of cucumber, we had discovered the East Arm was alive with great shoals of Smelt and being a small fish, nobody really bothered with them, apart from the odd freshwater fisherman who would take a few to use as Pike baits, we however, were just there for a bit of fun and returned all that we caught back to the water.

We used to fish very light rods, small hooks and the tiniest bits of worm compared to what were used to at the time, in effect fresh water tackle and we used to catch loads of them and what great fun they were to catch too. Of course it goes without saying that sometime our Smelt baits were intercepted by other species such as small school Bass, Red Mullet, the odd Joey Mackerel and the prehistoric looking beaked Garfish with its rows of tiny, but incredibly sharp teeth.

I continued fishing until I discovered girls, well one girl in particular (FT) and my fishing went to the wall for a good while, I still went now and again, but not as often as I used to, then one fateful day, Dad and I went down to the beach and were greeted by commercial boats fishing very close inshore and as far as the eye could see from east to west was a net just the other side of the marker buoys.

We stayed and fished but never caught a thing, we packed up and went home and after that apart from the odd trip for Mackerel in the summer, we never sea fished again, instead turning our interest and wallets to coarse fishing, which is a subject that would probably fill an entire book on its own.

We really did have that fateful, *One Last Cast* on the beach, but never knew it at the time.

The Farm

A trip to the farm always filled me with excitement, as it meant one thing, seeing Grandad, the farm is where Grandad worked for many, many years as the farm engineer and combine driver to name but a couple of the things he did here.

His workshop at the top of the farmyard was a place that always filled me with exhilaration, not only because of all the huge lorries and pieces of ever so complicated farm equipment that was normally always present as it underwent overhaul, repair or just a service in preparation for the upcoming tasks on the farm.

The workshop had a unique smell and I can still smell it to this day, a heady mixture of hydraulic fluid, oil, grease, the smoke from the welder, all mixed in with the smell of fresh cut grass and the inevitable plastering of animal muck and mud that seemed to get everywhere, its an unforgettable brew and one that I will never tire of, real country smells that you have to grow up with to truly appreciate.

The farm itself is nestled at the foot of a long Coombe in the South Downs and comprises of approximately one thousand acres of mixed arable and livestock farming, the farm is still with the same family today as it was when Grandad worked there, having passed through previous generations to the present day, like many farms in this modern age though, they have had to diversify in order to make the books balance, with farm tours, maize mazes, and coarse fishing ponds now all contributing to the farm.

Some of my earliest memories of going to farm are when on a Friday afternoon Mum, Nan, my Sister and I would go to the farmhouse to collect our weekly order of fresh baked, proper old fashioned crusty farmhouse bread, then after a quick chat with the farmers wife we would leave the bread in the car and walk up the yard to see Grandad in his workshop, you could hear him sometimes before his workshop even came into view as he swung a dirty great hammer and whacked the living daylights out of a stubborn bolt that wouldn't move, it was going to move come hell or high water and Grandad always won one way or another.

Whilst Mum & Nan chatted with Grandad, I would be there taking it all in, my eyes wandering around the workshop and studying the bits of tractor that were on the workshop floor, they always went back together though, my Sister and I would explore Grandad's workshop and would spend a fair amount of time playing in and around the inspection pit that was set into the floor, always being told to be careful and don't touch anything!

Grandad's workshop was his pride and joy, it was always clean and tidy and he knew exactly where everything was, it all had a place and it was all in its place, he could easily tell if someone had been in his workshop though, as they never put things back where they belonged and it did make him mad, im exactly the same, a real chip off the old block, I know where everything is in my workshop or in the lock-up up at the ponds I looked after, without even thinking about it I can direct people to a particular tool or piece of equipment, this is quite often to the amazement of the person whom im directing as they cannot quite get their head around this ability that I have inherited from Grandad.

Grandad used to have a saying that's always stuck with me *"Use the right right tool for the right job"* , even now when im working his voice will pop into my with this all important bit of advice, to which I say out loud *"yes Grandad"*, people do look at me a bit funny when I say it, but I know im sane.

Fridays were always a highlight of the week, as Nan used to come over from Steyning to do her weekly shop and Grandad used to come to the house after work to have his tea before taking Nan and the shopping home, his tea was quite often a nice pork pie and I used to sit next to him as he ate and say *"that looks nice Grandad"*, he would always cave in and give me a piece, not that he really minded of course, after tea was done we would sit nice and quiet and watch Out of Town or The Old Country by Jack Hargreaves on the telly, the intro music which to this day I struggle to listen to, after Jack finished, it was time for Nan & Grandad to go and time for me to go to bed.

Harvest time was a special time as we would go up to the top of the hills and watch Grandad drive the Combine as he harvested the Barley and Wheat, the Combine I remember the most is a huge, red, noisy Massey Ferguson with an enormous exposed flywheel on its side, an open cab and certainly no mod cons that the machines have these days, its was also considerably smaller than its modern brethren.

At the end of each working day Grandad would go home absolutely covered in dirt and dust from the crop he had been working that day and if he had been in the Barley fields, he was normally itching like crazy too as the Barley hairs got in everywhere.

The grain from the Combine was taken back to the farm in the same huge lorries that only weeks previous had been in pieces in the workshop, now they were all chugging along and working hard at earning their keep, now and again we /I would get a ride in the trailer which was a real treat, of course like so many things you are not allowed to do it these days on *"Health & Safety"* grounds.

The long rows of straw that came out the back of the Combine used to line the field like long rows of unintelligible text, this was not wasted though and once the Combine had finished the tractor and baler would move in to bale up all the straw. The bales were neatly stacked on flat bed lorries and trailers and taken back to the farm where it would later be used as animal bedding, very little went to waste.

Broken bales and small piles of straw that the baler couldn't get too were left on the field and burnt, as back then at the end of harvest, farms would burn the stubble fields and what a sight that used to be, for miles in the distance you could see plumes of thick smoke rising up from farms dotted around the Weald and Downs all burning the stubble off, of course this also presented an opportunity for us kids too and we used to make small camps from the broken bales and then watch them burn, walking over the freshly burnt fields was something we enjoyed too, the ground still so warm from the recent blaze that you could feel the heat permeating through your shoes and into your feet if you stood in any one place for too long, we would walk over the field kicking up the ash and taking in the smell, something that unfortunately people these days will never appreciate, the stubble burning and subsequent ploughing in also marked a sad time, as it normally fell at the end of the summer holidays which meant in just a few short days we would have to go back to school.

Lambing time each spring was always a fun time for us, although incredibly hard work for those on the farm, from an early age we would spend a lot of time each spring in the lambing shed, witnessing the births of these fluffy, cuddly lambs, we would bottle feed some of the orphan lambs never thinking what their future bore, both my Sister and I were exposed to the wonderment of a new life, equally we were also exposed to the harsh realities of life when a lamb was still born or died shortly after birth, these details were never hidden from us, we were always taught where our food came from and the harsh realities of it's production.

This was never ever more true than one trip to the farm where we looking out over a small field and watching the lambs jumping around and playing, when my Sister was asked what she wanted for dinner that evening, without hesitation she pointed towards a fluffy springtime lamb out in the field and said *"that one"*.

Later in the year it was shearing time and this always fascinated me, not just the process, but the speed at which the shearers worked, it was lightning fast, at the time I was too young to help out with packing the fleeces, but I was offered this opportunity a few years later and much to my now regret, I turned it down, what a fool I was, but I no doubt had my reasons at the time.

The farm was also one of the very first farms to offer farm tours, Grandad with his infinite skills was tasked with transforming an old farm trailer into a people transport that could be hitched behind a tractor and pulled around the farm so people could see how the farm worked. Grandad soon had the trailer built, sides, roof and steps all built and beautifully finished, seating was bales of straw.

We went on a couple of these tours around the farm, up past Grandad's workshop and the old rusty caterpillar tracked tractor that was left rusting in the hedge opposite having been made redundant by the latest Massey or Ford tractor, into the valley we went bouncing on the bales and up to the head, then along the track to the Dew Pond then back along the adjacent valley and back to the farm, all the time listening to a commentary from the farmers daughter.

There were so many good times at the farm, the barn dances, the barbecues in the field behind the farm house on a balmy summers evening, not any old barbecue though, these were huge as the centre piece was quite often a whole bullock being spit roasted over a massive bed of wood embers, the meat was carved off by the farmer and deposited onto slices of thick crusty bread covered in proper butter, no other sauces were needed, the beef and butter was more than enough, these masterpieces of the culinary world would be demolished whilst sitting on bales of straw in the evening sun, surrounded by family and friends, magical times.

Times have changed now and technology now does the work of so many former farmhands, the machinery is massive and the swath that Grandad would take in his Combine is now a quarter of that made by the modern machines, we quite often say that if Grandad could come back he wouldn't believe the size of the machines used today, nor the complexity of them and whilst the new machines are impressive, there is a part of me that yearns back to those days on the farm, sadly they will never return, except briefly in this tome and in my head.

At least with some of those times immortalised in print, future generations will be able to see how it used to be *"when I was a lad"*, in the same manner in which I was often told about the old days, when it was horse drawn carts, stooks and ricks, not tractors, bales and sheds.

Up The Clump

A local landmark that played a big part of my childhood was, The Clump, or to give it its proper name, Lancing Ring, but to the born and bred locals its simply, The Clump.

The clump is a small woodland comprised mainly of Beech, Ash & Sycamore, with an understorey of Hazel, Blackthorn, Spindle & Elder that nestles itself atop the South Downs close to home.

This area has been frequented by man for millennia, the track way that runs alongside it to the north is rumoured to be of Neolithic origin, there are Bronze age cross dykes just down the hill a short way to the north and in more *"recent"* times the Romans built a small Temple just to the west of the clump of trees, the remains of this Temple site can be be seen if you know where to look and its quite amazing how many people walk right over it without ever noticing it's there, its just another lump and bump in the ground as far as most are concerned.

I first started going to the clump on family afternoons out, not that often as we used to go to places like The Horseshoe & our Secret Spot in the main, but just now and again we would go up past the refuse tip that sat opposite the slope to the west of the clump to the trees perched on top of the hill.

The clump being so close to habitation had far more people around it than our normal haunts, which accounted for why we didn't come here that often.

The main time we went to the clump was after it had been snowing, easy to get to, lots of fun and a lot safer than trying to drive over to Steyning to go sledging and why would we when a perfectly suitable slope was on our doorstep?

Our sledge was one that Dad had built from scratch and the same one that I had used to propel myself at great speed down the Targets in Steyning, so with hats, gloves, big coats and the runners of the sledge suitably lubricated with a generous rubbing of candle wax, we would walk up to the clump from home for some fun in the snow.

The best run was to the east of the trees, a nice fairly wide, but flat path that had been worn my thousands of feet and the grass kept trimmed short by the resident Rabbits, so sat on the sledge, holding onto the rope handle it was time to go on the first run, with a gentle nudge I was off, sometimes on my own, sometimes tandem with Mum, Dad or my Sister, after a nice gentle run down we would approach the bottom of the slope which was bordered by a Blackthorn hedge, the only way to stop was to bail off the sledge or into the thorn thicket it was, bailing off hurt less.

Now at the bottom of the slope also lay a narrow cut between the hedge to left and the undergrowth to the right, this footpath having been used for hundreds of years was and still is rather hollowed out and in the winter when the snow ice was around it looked like something akin to the Cresta run, U shaped and coated in hard, shiny ice, for the brave or should that be, the stupid, this presented a challenge.

Laying the sledge on the ground at the top of the slope by the trees, you took a few steps backwards then ran towards the sledge, throwing yourself onto it's platform so you were laying down and going head first, with the extra momentum of the start you were off at a good lick already, god forbid anyone who got in the way.

Approaching the bottom of the slope and the narrow cut through you tried to steer the all important gap, if you got it right you lost all chance of steering as the shape and direction of the path now wholly dictated your destination, which if it went right, would see you extend your run by a good hundred yards or so, if you got it wrong, it often ended up with you being engulfed in a pile of snow and ice, a bundle of small human being rolling in concert with a heavy sledge and if it was a really good crash all you saw was sky, ground, sky, ground, sky, ground, of course being youngsters we did tend to bounce fairly well, so we would brush ourselves off, go back to the top of the hill and give it another try.

When I was in middle school I used to go to the clump with some school friends, some of whom I still see now, one day we went up there to play, but we had some special toys with us that had come from France.

A week or so earlier we had been on a school trip to Dieppe in France on a school trip, now back then one of the highlights of a French trip was the opportunity to buy French Bangers, basically small fireworks that looked all the world like sticks of dynamite, we knew we were not supposed to have them and we were undoubtedly too young to legally buy them, the shopkeepers sold them to us anyway.

So we didn't get caught with them by the teachers we smuggled these things back to Blighty hidden in our socks and pants, we succeeded and got them home undiscovered, now to stash them at home where they would not be found by our parents.

A few weeks after the trip "the boys" arranged to meet up at the clump with the bangers, most of us had purchased the smaller ones that were about an inch or so long as they were easier to hide on our persons, and we now had great fun setting these off in the woods, but a couple of the boys had bought some of the bigger bangers and boy did they go bang, but we wanted to do more than just set them off, so we located a small tree stump of perhaps a few inches in diameter and wondered what would happen if we put a big banger underneath it?

First off this stump was still fairly solid in the ground, we couldn't move it, we excavated a small hole beneath it, put in a banger, lit it and ran, when we were what we thought was a safe distance we stopped and turned around ready to view the results of our experiment. The banger went off with a huge bang and the force of the explosion lifted the small stump clear of the ground, you can imagine the excited laughs of a group of small boys.

Having a few bangers left we thought we would try some more stump removal, I cant remember if we were successful or not, but the vision of that first stump leaping into the air has never left me, we never did give any thought though to what would have happened if one of those bangers had gone off when we were smuggling them back tucked away in our clothing.

While I was still at middle school I used to occasionally go to a friends house on a Sunday morning, he used to live a few hundred yards away from the bottom of the hill that the clump sat on and we used to traipse up there and just mess around for a few hours climbing trees and generally having fun before it was time to go home for Sunday lunch.

Sometimes though we would go and play in the old chalk pit that lay to the east of the clump, it wasn't a particularly big pit, but it was quite steep and one side of the pit made a great slide, as you could clearly see by the slick surface made by countless people sliding down it, albeit not a clean slide down as it was quite mucky with mud and chalk being liberated each time you went down.

One particular time we were up there messing around as kids do, I was up and down the chalk non stop and was absolutely plastered, head to toe in chalk and crud, my friend and I were always told to be back at our respective houses in time for lunch and I can recall looking at my watch in horror as I saw the time, I was seriously late for lunch, we left the chalk pit in a hurry and went, my friend having the distinct advantage of not having very far to go and me with a bit further to go with my heart in my mouth fearing a right ticking off when I got home.

Running as fast as my little legs would take me, I ran homewards over the lower slopes of the hill towards home, when I got there, I rang the doorbell and braced myself for the tongue lashing that was going to shortly happen, Mum opened the door, glared at me, looked me up and down and just burst into laughter as she looked at the sorry state of her eldest stood there, covered from top to bottom in chalk, I didn't know whether to laugh or cry, once she stopped laughing she asked if I had had a good time, I replied *"yes"*, *"well, that's all that matters then"* she replied and that was the end of it, although she never did let me forget that one.

When I reached secondary school the clump still played a part in my life, at school we would do the dreaded cross country run as part of our PE class, this included running up to the clump from school, going right up to it's northern edge, round that, then back down the western edge and back to school, it was exhausting and I hated it, I wasn't a runner, I was good at rugby and field athletics, but running, distance or otherwise was not for me.

So on these cross country runs, a few of us had the idea of cutting the distance we had to go a bit short, we would go up to the clump, then when the teachers were not looking, we would cut through the woods to the western side, hide for a bit, then as the stragglers came past we would emerge from the woods and have a leisurely jog down hill and back to school, of course we thought we had been very clever and inventive in our little wheeze, but the teachers were of course more than switched on to it.

We thought we had got away with it as nothing was said, but on one fateful day as we emerged from the woods, there waiting for us was the sports master, we had been caught red handed, our penance, go and do it again and no cheating this time, lesson learned the hard way.

Out of school and as a teenager I would still go to the clump, not to blow things up this time, but to fly radio controlled model aircraft. The clump has a wonderful south west facing slope that is just perfect for for model gliders, I used to have a number of different models that I had built from scratch, from large one hundred inch wingspan floaters for light winds and calm conditions to fast, sleek aerobatic gliders for when the wind blew hard, it was great to fly up there with a superb view down over home then over Sompting Brooks towards Worthing and the sea beyond.

Into adulthood and I still go up there now and again, I was involved with a local conservation group for a few years and we used to meet once a month at the clump and help maintain the area, nothing overly strenuous, just cutting back overgrown paths mainly, but I had to give that up when I fell ill in 2016, hopefully when im fixed and fit again I can go back and help out once more as it was great fun.

Chanctonbury

Chanctonbury Ring is a large hill that rises to approximately seven hundred feet above sea level and lays more or less mid way between Steyning and Washington in West Sussex, it's very much a local landmark due to it's ring of trees on the very top of the hill that can be seen for miles in many directions, we always knew when we were home from holiday or a day out when we saw "Chanky" in the distance.

The ring of trees was originally planted in 1760 by Charles Goring, an ancestor of the current custodians of the Wiston Estate, the trees were mainly Beech and were planted within the boundary of the Iron Age earthworks, the remains of which are unmistakable, also within the boundary of the fort are the remains of two Roman Temples and evidence of the Roman occupation abounds with pieces of broken roof tile everywhere, there is plenty of evidence of their meals too with Oyster and Cockle shells littering the area betraying the Romans love of seafood.

When were were kids Mum and Dad would take us up Chanctonbury on a fairly regular basis, it's somewhere they, my Sister and I really enjoyed, as there was always so much to do, on the way to top and not long after leaving the car park you come to the swinging ropes, these are a series of ropes put high up in the Beech trees for people to swing on, they are unofficial, but there is very much a tradition of the ropes being here, certainly all of my life they have been put there and the same being true back in Dad's day too.

The Beech trees are glorious old specimens, hundreds and hundreds of years old, some so old that they have Ash trees growing in the cracks and crevices left by broken branches and large bracket fungi emerging from their trunks like natural shelves, the roots of the trees in some places have been hollowed out over the years by thousands of small feet and they now over hang and create what we latterly called Hobbit Caves, so deep that an adult can lay outstretched in them.

We always stopped at the ropes for a little while and had a play on the ropes and still do, well you really are only as old as you feel and of course,it would be rude not to go and have a play.

The climb up to the top of the hill always seemed to take forever and day to do, the steep sided, well eroded path at times felt like it was closing in on you, but there were always distractions to break up the climb, such as climbing the sides of the path and then walking over the trees that had fallen and now lay over the path as impromptu bridges to nowhere.

Even when we got to the top of the path we still had a way to go before we got to the actual ring of trees, now out in the open, the path widened considerably as it wound it's way along the top of the hill, woodland to our right and farmland to the left, knowing people had traversed this path for millennia often made and indeed often makes me wonder how many thousands of feet had travelled the same path over the years?

Approaching the brow of a small rise we carefully navigate ourselves over the cattle grid, ever fearful of a wrong step and our legs disappearing down between the steel bars, we are now on the grazing land and the glory that is Chanctonbury Ring lays dead ahead.

As we walk along the top of the ridge we have commanding views to the north over the Weald and right off into the distance we can see the North Downs around Dorking in Surrey, to the south we can see along the coast from the Seven Sisters to Bognor and on really clear days as far as the Isle of Wight.

We arrive at the ring and it doesn't take long to climb up the earthworks and sit on the top, sat there now having a much needed drink and perhaps a bite to eat in the shade of an old Beech tree with the inner ring behind us. The inside of the ring always seemed to be a dark and foreboding place when I was younger, mainly because of the lack of sunlight filtering through the canopy to the ground, but also probably because of the stories and folklore that abounds about this place.

One story in particular that Mum and Dad used to tell my Sister and I was the one where it was said that if you held your breath and ran around the ring three times, then the Devil would appear, we took it all in and even tried running around the ring whilst holding our breath, we never got more than a few tens of feet before our lungs were bursting and we gasped for air, of course if you did mange to run round the ring three times, the Devil may well appear, but so would your ancestors whom you would soon be joining as you would very much be brown bread.

Of course no trip to Chanctonbury was ever complete without a trip to the Dew Pond that lay at the western end of the ridge, the walk to the pond used to fill me with questions when I saw all of the lumps and bumps in the ground, I now know these to be Cross Dykes and the remains of barrows that were created back in the Iron age, once at the Dew Pond we would sit for a while and just take it in and study the wealth of insects that called it home all this way up on top of the South Downs, Dragon and Damsel flies, Pond Skaters, Water Boatmen and the occasional Frog, we would look at the tracks left in the marginal mud by Birds and animals where they had come for a much needed drink.

The way down from the top of Chanctonbury was without doubt the best bit of any trip up there, because as anyone who knows the place will tell you, the side of the hill is very, very steep and covered in loose chalk and leaves, the hill is so steep that its nigh on impossible to go down the side standing up, so the only feasible way down is on your backside, we all did it, Mum, Dad, Sister and even my Nan at seventy years old went down the side of Chanctonbury on her bum, it just had to be done.

When I was a teenager my cousin from America came to stay for a number of weeks and we took her to Chanctonbury, now she hails from Florida which is as flat as a pancake, she had never seen anything as tall as Chanctonbury except in photographs, but she climbed all the way to the top then came down the steep side on her rear, her jeans were filthy dirty, ripped and holed, did she care, not a bit of it, and all these years later she still has those jeans in her wardrobe as a reminder of her trip to England.

Even now when I go to Chanctonbury I come down the steep side, not all the time, but just sometimes for prosperity, certainly when I used to take my two nephews up there, we would come down on our backsides, so that's at least four generations of our family that have ploughed ridge and furrow on those slopes with our derrières, we didn't always come down on our rears, sometimes my nephews and I would abseil down the slope, not only for a change, but to show them a safer way to descend a steep slope, it was still fun, but not quite as much as thundering down on your rear.

My adulthood trips to Chanctonbury are a lot more subdued these days, I much prefer for most of the time, to just take my time and take in my surroundings, listening for and watching the Roe & Fallow Deer that frequent the area, perhaps a little bit of basic tracking to see if I can follow their path through the woods, normally I do ok until I get to a spot where they are much better adapted at going on than I.

As you walk up and down there are all manner of birds to see and hear, Woodpeckers happily tapping away, Jays calling, the mew of a Buzzard overhead and the panicked flap of the Wood Pigeon as you intrude into its world, at the top you can see evidence of the ever present rabbit population, with droppings on the grass and runs disappearing into the bramble thickets, you sometimes find the remains of bunny that became a Foxes meal when it didn't quite run fast enough, the Pheasant cackling as it runs away from you over the field opposite and the glorious sound of the Skylark overhead, all of this sometimes broken by the whistle of a man made bird as a high performance glider from the local gliding field swoops overhead using the updraught of the south west wind on the southerly slope to stay aloft.

Of course once back at the bottom of the hill and regardless of age you have to have a go on the swinging ropes before heading down the path and back to the small car park and home, tired but happy.

Chanctonbury Ring was unfortunately devastated in the great storm of 1987, which saw many of the beautiful old trees toppled like dominoes, one positive from the carnage caused by the raw power of nature was the revealing of masses of archaeology that had lain undisturbed for years, that was now visible under the root plates of the fallen trees, information on what was found and its importance can be found online via a simple search for Chanctonbury Ring Roman Remains.

Once the archaeologists had finished the Estate replanted the ring and fenced it off to afford the saplings some protection and let them grow safe from grazing animals and humans, it has only been in very recent years that the trees have grown sufficiently to allow the removal of the fence and allow free access to the the ring once more.

So if you are in the area, why not take a trip to the top, look at the remains of past civilisation and the stunning vista that the height of the hill affords you, try if you dare to summon the Devil, then slide down the hill on your rear, then once you have dusted yourself off, go for a swing on the ropes, you'll be glad you did.

Finally

Thank you for taking the time to read my scribblings, I do hope you have found them interesting, informative and hopefully a little entertaining, what my family will think of some of the antics I used to get up to I don't know, but im sure they will tell me.

There are of course many experiences that I have not written about and some that will never get written about, if the mood takes me in the future, I might just well sit down and write part two, heaven only knows what people will think at some of those adventures.

As I mentioned at the very beginning, I have written this book, not only for prosperity, but as a mental release during a particularly hard time in my life that at the moment is showing no sign of having an end point.

I do feel it is important that people understand and talk about mental health, there has been a considerable amount of improvement in the understanding and treatment of mental health conditions in recent years, your mental well being is as important as your physical health and it certainly doesn't carry the stigma that it did just a few years ago, please don't be afraid to look for help if you need it, its out there, all you have to do is ask.

Perhaps if you are one of those people who are struggling, then why not pick up pen and paper and write a few words yourself, its really not as daunting as you might think once you get going and it really does help.

By writing down these memories and stories, I have found some of the release and distraction that I sought, I long to be able to get back outside and into nature where I belong, only then do I feel that I will be somewhat at peace with myself again, that time will of course come and it's a worthy goal, until I can get there though, I will content myself with looking at nature through the window, watching the Squirrel scoot along the top of the fence panels between us and next door, the Blue Tits flitting around starting to think about nesting as spring approaches and winter finally loses its icy grip, the hover Sparrows as I call them as they search for food along the eaves of the house and hovering like a hummingbird when they locate a tasty morsel and the cheeky Robin who sits outside my window singing his heart out most days, there are many ways to experience nature, being out there is obviously the best, but if you cannot get there for whatever reason that may be, nature will always come to you, even in the middle of a city or town, nature will be with you.

Finally, and in the words of John Denver, I will leave you with this;

" Thank God I'm A Country Boy "

Printed in Great Britain
by Amazon

34997532R00066